Camp Cookin'

Mary Ann Kerl

3

Dedicated to

my husband Bob,
and our two sons,
Jim and Jeff,
and in memory
of two dear friends,
Wanda and Martin Mummert,
for giving me
such enjoyable camping trips

Acknowledgment

A special thank you to the publishing companies who first printed the materials in this book and either returned residual rights back to me or published my recipes and materials for one-time use only.

Two companies that I'm especially grateful to are *Northeast Outdoors* and *Camperways,* who contributed the most materials to this book. Some of the other companies include various publications from Tower Press and The House of White Birches, Inc.

Forword

Mary Ann Kerl has put together this book with
the cook in mind.

She has managed to combine some really delicious
recipes with ease of preparation and ease of clean up.

It is, as she says, "......a lot more fun to play
in nice clean lake water than dirty old dish water."

Preface

This book was nearly thirty years in the making.

Over the years I've experimented with numerous recipes and projects especially for camping. Friends, relatives and strangers gave me some great ideas for camping enjoyment in addition to my own.

Notice our camp projects include homemade camp equipment, made in minutes for only pennies. Plus, we've developed a pizza that can be baked in our camp oven made from a cardboard box.

Also examine how our nutritious recipes are simple to prepare. They were developed so the camp chef can give campers hearty meals to satisfy outdoor appetites and still provide time for the chef to join in camp activities like swimming, hiking and boating.

This book also features projects to do at home. Make a child's backpack with a towel and a couple washcloths by simply following our instructions. We also have an excellent way to wash and clean your sleeping bag. In addition, we've included enjoyable projects for active camp kids.

Regardless, if you're a beginner or advanced camper, you're bound to enjoy our clever camp recipes and projects. Go for it!

Table of Contents

Unit 1 **Recipes For Homemade Camp Equipment**
    Chapter 1   Camp Oven   17
    Chapter 2   Camp Stove   21
    Chapter 3   Camp Toaster   23

Unit 2 **Recipes For Store-Purchased Camp Equipment**
    Chapter 4   Dutch Oven   29
    Chapter 5   Cast-Iron Skillet   35

Unit 3 **Recipes For Easy-To-Make Camp Dishes**
    Chapter 6   Main Dish Camp Recipes   41
    Chapter 7   It'll Look Like . . .   47

Unit 4 **Recipes For Easy-Clean-Up**
    Chapter 8   Paper Bag Breakfast   51
    Chapter 9   Throw-Away Dishes   55
    Chapter 10   Disposable Salad Bowl   61

Unit 5 **Recipes For Fall/Winter**
    Chapter 11   Hot & Hearty Winter Meals   65
    Chapter 12   Warm Winter Stews   69
    Chapter 13   Hot & Hearty Desserts   75
    Chapter 14   Snow Ice-Cream   79

Unit 6 **Recipes For Spring/Summer**
    Chapter 15   Cold & Clever Meals   85
    Chapter 16   Cold & Clever Vegetables   91
    Chapter 17   Main Dish Camp Salads   99
    Chapter 18   July 4th Recipes   103

Unit 7   Recipes For Bread Products

Chapter 19	Camp Biscuits	111
Chapter 20	Muffins	117
Chapter 21	Beer Breads	121

Unit 8   Camping Projects

Chapter 22	Clean Your Sleeping Bag	125
Chapter 23	Making A Child's Backpack	129
Chapter 24	Keeping Camp Kids Happy	137

Unit 1
Recipes For Making Your Own Camp Equipment

Chapter 1   Make A Camp Oven In Minutes!

Have no camp oven? Make one with a cardboard box. It costs only pennies and works great! See p. 145-147

Items needed: cardboard box, string or one large rubber band, plastic oven wrap, knife, 4 or 5 coat hangers, oven thermometer, pliers and a small charcoal grill.

To begin: cut off flaps from the cardboard box open end. Then cut a hole in the opposite side of the box, making it slightly smaller than the grill. For the oven rack, use a broiler rack or make one.

To make an oven rack: use pliers to straighten the coat hangers into long pieces. Then cut the straightened hangers about three inches longer than the box width. Stick each end of the hangers through the box in a straight line. Space hangers about 1½ to 2 inches apart for proper support and bend ends so they will not slide through the box.

To hang the oven thermometer: place another hanger wire through the box several inches above and to one side of the rack you just made. To use, place the product to be baked on the oven rack. Cover the open end of the box with plastic oven wrap and secure with string or a large rubber band. The large bands that come in a box of tinker toys works nicely for a medium-sized box. The oven wrap can be purchased in most grocery or department stores for a few cents.

Next: place the oven over a bed of hot charcoal in your small charcoal grill. It will take only a couple minutes for the thermometer to record the temperature inside the oven. Regulate the temperature accordingly by raising or lowering the box.

All kinds of foods can be cooked in this oven. We've developed a pizza especially for outdoor camp cooking that can be baked with your homemade camp oven. Simply follow our recipe on the next page.

CLEVER CAMP PIZZA

Crust ingredients:
3 cups biscuit mix
3/4 cup milk

Sauce ingredients:
1/2 pound sliced pepperoni
1 cup mozzarella cheese, grated or sliced thin
1 8 ounce can tomato sauce
1/2 teaspoon basil
1/2 teaspoon oregano

Directions for crust:
Compare ratio measurements of biscuit mix and milk with measurements above. Use measurements given on your box if they differ from above. Stir biscuit mix and milk together. Shape into a ball and place on greased or non-stick cookie sheet. With clean hands, press dough into a thin crust. (Dip hands in flour first if dough is sticky. Rub hands with a little shortening if dough is dry.)

Directions for sauce: Mix spices, basil and oregano, with tomato sauce in the can to save dishes. Spread seasoned sauce onto crust. Add sliced pepperoni and top with grated cheese.

Place prepared pizza in camp oven and bake at 425 degrees F. Regulate the temperature by raising or lowering the box. Bake for 20 to 30 minutes or until crust is nicely brown and cheese is melted.

Chapter 2   Camp Stove

Stop. Don't throw that empty tuna can away and save an empty coffee can too. For about ten cents, recycle these cans into a camp stove!

Step 1: Make the burner with either a 6 ounce tuna can and a 2 pound coffee can, or a 12 ounce tuna can and a 3 pound coffee can. Wash and dry the tuna can and fill with sawdust that can be obtained at a local lumber yard. If sawdust isn't available, pencil sharpener shavings may be used. See p. 148

After filling the tuna can with sawdust or pencil shavings, place it in a 200 degree F. oven for one hour. This dries the sawdust or pencil shavings so the melted paraffin won't foam when poured over the sawdust or shavings.

Next remove the tuna can from the oven. If you are using a small tuna can, pour one quarter-pound block of melted paraffin over the dry sawdust or pencil shavings. If, however, you're using a large size tuna can, use two quarter-pound blocks of paraffin. Then allow your homemade camp burner to cool and harden.

Step 2: Make the heat regulator, using the tuna can lid. Simply cut out the bottom straight section of a wire clothes hanger, bend in a U-shape and solder the hanger ends to the can lid. This lid may be used to extinguish the fire when finished cooking as well as regulating the heat.

Step 3: Make the stove with the coffee can. Open one side for the main vent. To do this, use pliers to cut the open edge of the can several times in a four-inch area. Roll the cut area half way toward the top of the can. You'll also need some smaller vents To make these, take a soda pop can opener and punch holes, about three inches apart, around the top side of the coffee can. See p. 149

To use the burner, begin by lighting the burner. Simply hold the can upside down and place a lighted match underneath the can. After you start a small flame, turn the can sideways and slowly rotate until you have a full flame. Then place the burner (tuna can) inside the stove (coffee can) and adjust the heat with the regulator lid. For low heat, place the lid three-fourths over the flame. For medium heat, place the lid one-half over the flame. For high heat, simply don't use the lid.

When you pack this stove for your next camping trip, don't take any steel wool pads along. You won't need them. The soot goes on the inside of the coffee can, not on the pots and pans you set on this stove.

And think of all the foods you can heat with this camp stove. You can warm up soups, stews and hot dogs with it. Or you can sizzle eggs, potatoes and bacon with the stove. You can even perk your morning cup of coffee with this stove Enjoy!

Chapter 3   **Camp Toaster**

Tired of going without toast on camp trips? Make the camp toaster featured here. It's portable, lightweight and compact and can be made in minutes! See p. 150

Materials needed: 3 pound coffee can, wire coat hanger, hammer, nail, pliers and a paint scraper.

To begin: make vent holes in the bottom of the 3 pound coffee can, using a hammer and a large nail. To do this, pound the nail into the coffee can closed end again and again. Make a bunch of holes this way, spacing them an inch apart. Next, shorten the coffee can to a usable length; cut the coffee can all the way around the first indented ridge, using a hammer and a heavy paint scraper. Hold the coffee can secure and hammer the sharp edge of the scraper into the coffee can indented ridge. After doing this all the way around the ridge, discard the part with the open end.

The excess coffee can material is cut off for heat regulation. By having just a couple inches of overhang from the toaster top, the bread can be toasted quickly over a campfire, charcoal grill or camp stove. For safety: turn the bottom sharp edge of the coffee can back with pliers by twisting the sharp end of the cut ridge flat against the inside of the coffee can. That way the bottom edge is smooth and safe.

Make toast holders from: a coat hanger. Using pliers, cut two 12-inch pieces of wire from the hanger and bend each wire piece into a V shape. Invert and slip the two ends of the V shape wire into two of the vent holes. Place the inverted V wires on opposite sides of the coffee can.

To use the toaster: place two slices of bread, one on each inverted V holder, and toast, turning once, until nicely browned on both sides.

With our recipes, you can use this toaster for breakfast or brunch or dinner or lunch while at camp. Try our tasty recipes that follow.

Toast Recipes
(for Breakfast or Brunch)

PEANUT BUTTER SPECIAL

1/4 cup peanut butter
2 teaspoons honey
2 tablespoons pineapple juice
1/4 cup cream cheese

In mixing bowl, mix peanut butter, honey, pineapple juice and cream cheese thoroughly. To serve, spread on warm toast. Serves 4.

APPLE BUTTER SPECIAL

1 apple
1/4 cup apple butter or jam
2 tablespoons vanilla yogurt
1/4 cup slivered almonds

Wash, core and dice apple and place in small mixing bowl. Add apple butter or jam, vanilla yogurt and slivered almonds. Stir. To serve, spread on warm toast. Serves 4.

CARMEL CINNAMON TOAST

1/4 cup brown sugar
2 teaspoons cinnamon
1/8 teaspoon clove

In a small mixing bowl, stir ingredients together. Toast one side of bread on camp toaster. Spread untoasted bread sides with butter or margarine. Sprinkle spiced brown sugar mixture on top. Place bread slices back on camp toaster and toast until sugar mixture is bubbly and hot. Serves 4.

CREAMY ORANGE TOAST

1/4 cup sour cream
1 tablespoon orange juice
1 tablespoon grated orange rind
1/4 teaspoon nutmeg

In a small mixing bowl, stir sour cream, orange juice, orange rind and nutmeg together. To serve, spread orange mixture on warm toast. Serves 4.

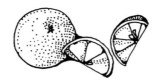

Toast Recipes
(for Dinner or Lunch)

BEST BEAN DELIGHT

1 24 ounce can pork 'n beans
1 tablespoon barbecue sauce
1/4 cup green pepper, chopped
1/4 cup onion, chopped
1/4 cup stuffed olives, sliced

Toast four slices of bread on camp toaster. Place above
ingredients in small saucepan. Stir until ingredients are
coated with barbecue sauce. Stirring occasionally, cook over
medium heat about 5 to 10 minutes or until ingredients are
piping hot. Pour hot beans on top of 4 toasted bread slices.
(Green pepper and onion will be crisp.) Serves 4.

BROCCOLI AND HAM

4 ham slices, cooked
1 10 ounce package broccoli spears, cooked
1 10¾ ounce can cheese soup
1/3 cup milk

Toast four bread slices and place a slice of heated ham and
two or three hot cooked broccoli spears on top of each toast
slice. Mix cheese soup with milk and heat in saucepan over
medium heat. When piping hot, pour cheese soup mixture
over ham and broccoli on toast. Recipe serves 4.

CHICKEN AND GREEN BEANS

4 servings of sliced chicken, cooked
1   14½ ounce can string green beans
1   10¾ ounce can cream of mushroom soup
1/4 cup green bean juice, reserved
1 cup grated cheddar cheese

Toast four slices of bread on camp toaster. Put heated
chicken slices on top of toast. Heat and drain green beans,
reserving ¼ cup of juice. Put drained green beans on top of
chicken. Mix mushroom soup with bean juice and heat in a
saucepan over medium heat. When piping hot, pour mixture
over toast, chicken and beans. Sprinkle grated cheddar
cheese on top. Serves 4.

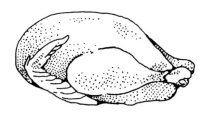

Unit 2
Recipes For Store Purchased Camp Equipment

Chapter 4   **Dutch Oven**

Grab a Dutch oven for your next campout. This utensil is great for making these easy one-pot camp dishes. All of our recipes were developed especially for Dutch oven cooking via the hole-in-the-ground method.

This method of camp cooking is easy. First, dig a pit in the ground. Make the pit larger and deeper than the Dutch oven. A note of safety: Select a site that is pure mineral soil and not full of humus. A humus site can cause a forest or range fire.

Next line the pit with small stones. Do this to prevent the loss of heat through the ground. Using charcoal or twigs, build a fire in the pit. Let the fire burn an hour or longer, until there is nothing left but hot coals. Carefully remove some of the hot coals and set aside. Then rake the remaining coals with a stick to make about one or two inches of hot coal ashes.

Now the prepared Dutch oven dish can be put in the pit. To do this, simply set the Dutch oven on the hot coal ashes. Then put the removed hot coals on top of the Dutch oven lid. Pour the fresh dirt gently back in the pit, covering the Dutch oven completely. Make the dirt blanket about four to six inches thick to give good insulation. Bake according to directions given in following recipes. Different dishes vary.

PORK CHOPS & STUFFING

8 thick pork chops
10 slices of bread
1/4 cup onion, chopped
1/2 cup water
1/2 teaspoon poultry seasoning
margarine or butter
2 cups mushroom soup
1 1/2 cups water

Place pork chops in Dutch oven. In a bowl, place bread (torn into crumbs), chopped onion, 1/2 cup of water (rest of water will be used later) and poultry seasoning to make stuffing. Toss with a fork. Place stuffing mix on top of pork chops. Put dabs of margarine, to desired taste, on top of stuffing.

In a bowl, stir soup and 1½ cups water together until well mixed. Pour this mixture over stuffing in Dutch oven. Cover with lid. Bake in pit for two to three hours or until meat is nicely tender. Serves 8.

BEEF COKE ROAST

2 12 ounce Cokes
6 to 8 pounds beef roast
pepper

Place beef roast in Dutch oven. Pour Coke over roast. Sprinkle pepper, to desired taste, over roast. Cover roast with Dutch oven lid and bake in pit for four to six hours or until meat is nicely tender. Serves 8.

GOURMET SWISS STEAK

8 1 inch thick serving size slices of round steak
2 envelopes dry onion soup mix
2 cups canned mushrooms
2 green peppers
1 12 ounce can tomatoes
1/3 cup steak sauce
pepper to taste
2 tablespoons chopped parsley

Place steak in Dutch oven. Sprinkle dry soup over steak.
Drain mushrooms and wash and slice green peppers. Place
prepared vegetables over steak. In a bowl, mix tomatoes,
steak sauce and pepper together. Pour this mixture over
steaks and vegetables. Sprinkle chopped parsley on top.
Cover and bake in pit for 2 to 3 hours or until meat and
vegetables are nicely tender. Serves 8.

BEST BAKED BEANS

1 pound dry Navy beans
6 cups water
2 onions, quartered
1/3 cup ketchup
1/4 cup molasses
1 tablespoon vinegar
1 teaspoon mustard

Cover beans with water in Dutch oven. Let soak overnight
or for several hours until beans double in size. Add prepared
onions. In bowl, mix ketchup, molasses, vinegar and mustard
together. Add to beans and onions. Stir. Bake in pit for 6 to
8 hours or until beans are nicely tender. Serves 6 to 8.

LAMB CHOPS WITH ZUCCHINI

1/2 cup water
8 thick lamb chops
2 large onions, sliced
8 zucchini, sliced thick
1 teaspoon pepper
1/2 teaspoon garlic powder
2 teaspoons basil leaves, crumbled

Pour water in Dutch oven. Trim fat from lamb chops. Place
trimmed chops in Dutch oven with water. Place sliced onions
and zucchini on top of chops. Sprinkle pepper, garlic powder
and crumbled basil leaves over lamb chops, onions and
zucchini. Bake in pit for 1 to 2 hours or until meat and
vegetables are nicely tender. Serves 8.

BARBECUED CHICKEN WITH POTATOES

1 whole cleaned chicken
1 cup ketchup
1/3 cup Worcestershire sauce
1 tablespoon chili powder
1 teaspoon onion powder or salt
1/2 teaspoon garlic powder or salt
2 tablespoons brown sugar
1 cup water
8 potatoes

Wash chicken and place in Dutch oven. In a bowl, mix all of
the other ingredients, except the potatoes, together. Pour
this mixture over chicken. Wash potatoes, scrubbing skins
thoroughly. Place potatoes around chicken. Bake in pit for 5
to 7 hours or until meat and vegetables are nicely tender.
Serves 8.

ROAST HAM WITH SWEET POTATOES

1 12 pound ham
8 sweet potatoes
1/3 cup dark corn syrup
2 tablespoons soy sauce
1/4 teaspoon ginger
1 tablespoon cornstarch

Place ham in Dutch oven. Wash or peel sweet potatoes. Put
cleaned potatoes around ham. In a small bowl, mix corn
syrup, soy sauce, ginger and cornstarch together. Pour
mixture over ham. Cover and bake in pit for 6 to 8 hours or
until meat and vegetables are nicely tender. Serves 8.

Chapter 5   Cast Iron Skillet

At last. We have it. Our special skillet suppers are bound to please everyone, including the camp chef.

With just one pan, tadaaah!--the skillet!, you can prepare our camp dishes with ease. Serve with a bowl of fruit and milk for a complete nutritious camp meal.

Notice these one-dish skillet recipes are economical too. Featuring inexpensive foods, our skillet suppers are combined with just the right amount of seasoning for a great taste every time. That's why our skillet recipes please even picky camp eaters. So the next time you camp out, grab a skillet (and our recipes) for an extra special camp outing.

CRAFTY CHICKEN & ASPARAGUS

1 5 ounce can boned chicken
1 10¾ ounce can cream of asparagus
1 teaspoon basil leaves
1/2 teaspoon oregano
pepper to taste
1 15 ounce can carrots, undrained

Drain chicken and place in skillet. In a bowl, mix soup with spices and add to skillet. Pour can of carrots with juice in frying pan. Stirring occasionally, cook over medium heat for 5 to 10 minutes or until ingredients are piping hot. Serve over a thick, crisp bed of potato chips. Delicious! Serves 4.

Sweet Sausage Supper

1 tablespoon margarine or butter
1 12 ounce package sausage links, cooked
1 17ounce can sweet potatoes
1 8 ounce can pineapple slices
1 tablespoon brown sugar

Melt margarine or butter in skillet. Add sausage links and fry
over medium heat until browned. Push sausage to pan edges.
Place sweet potatoes in middle of pan. Put pineapple slices,
well drained, on top of potatoes. Sprinkle brown sugar on
top of sweet potatoes and pineapple. Cover and cook for
about 5 minutes or until brown sugar is melted and bubbly
and ingredients are piping hot. Serves 4 to 6.

SUPER SKILLET EGGS

1/4 cup margarine or butter
8 bread slices
1 cup sharp cheddar cheese, grated
5 eggs, well beaten
1/3 cup milk
salt and pepper to taste
1/4 teaspoon dry mustard
1 cup cooked ham, diced

Melt margarine or butter in skillet. Cut bread into large cubes and add to melted margarine. Fry bread in skillet until nicely browned. In a small bowl, mix cheese, eggs, milk, salt, pepper and dry mustard together. Add ham and pour mixture into frying pan. Stirring occasionally, cover and cook, over low heat, until eggs are light and fluffy and nicely set. Serves 4 to 6.

TASTY TUNA TOAST

1 6 ounce can tuna
1 10¾ ounce can cheese soup
1 15 ounce can peas
1 teaspoon seasoned salt

Drain tuna and place in skillet; lightly flake with fork. Add cheese soup, peas (undrained) and seasoned salt. Stir until tuna and peas are coated with soup. Stirring occasionally, cover and cook, over medium to low heat, for 5 to 10 minutes or until ingredients are piping hot. Serve over toasted, crusty French bread slices. Serves 4 to 6.

GOURMET SKILLET WIENERS

1/4 cup onion, chopped
1/4 cup green pepper, chopped
1/4 cup margarine or butter
1 27 ounce can sauerkraut
1 16 ounce can small, whole potatoes
1 14½ ounce can string beans
1 one-pound package wieners
American cheese

Saute onion and green pepper in margarine or butter. Drain
sauerkraut, potatoes and string beans. Place well drained
vegetables in frying pan. Stirring occasionally, cook
vegetables for 5 to 10 minutes, over medium heat, or until
ingredients are piping hot.

Slit wieners lengthwise, being careful not to cut completely
through the wiener. Cut cheese into long, thin strips. Place
cheese strips into slashed wieners. Place cheese-filled
wieners on top of vegetables in skillet. Checking occasionally
to make sure vegetables don't burn, cover and cook over
medium heat until wieners are piping hot and cheese is
melted. Serves 4 to 6.

SPECIAL SPANISH RICE

1 tablespoon chili powder
1 teaspoon paprika
pepper to taste
1 pound hamburger
1 6 ounce can tomato paste
1 10¾ ounce can tomato puree
1 cup water
1½ cups minute rice
1 15¼ ounce can corn
1/2 cup mushrooms, chopped
1/2 cup celery, thinly sliced crosswise

With clean hands, mix first three ingredients into hamburger.
Brown seasoned hamburger in skillet. Add tomato paste,
tomato puree, water, rice and corn (undrained). Stir. Add
chopped mushrooms and sliced celery. Stirring occasionally,
cover and cook, over medium heat, for about 15 minutes or
until ingredients are well heated and rice is fluffy and tender.
Serves 4 to 6.

HOT & HEARTY TUNA

1 6 ounce can tuna
1 10¾ ounce can of mushroom soup
1 teaspoon pepper
1 cup cheddar cheese, grated

Drain tuna and place in skillet. Add mushroom soup, pepper
and grated cheddar cheese. Stir. Stirring occasionally, cover
and cook, over medium to low heat, for 5 to 10 minutes or
until ingredients are piping hot and cheese is melted and
bubbly. Serve over a bed of potato chips or toasted and
crusty slices of French bread. Serves 4 to 6.

Unit 3
Recipes Featuring Easy To Make Dishes

Chapter 6   Oh, So Easy Main Dish Camp Recipes

No longer does the camp chef have to miss out on fun activities at camp. Now you can use our newly developed camp recipes featuring easy preparation meals that taste absolutely great.

We've got several main dish recipes with tips for extras for hearty eaters! Plus, there's some delicious vegetable and fruit recipes to accompany the main dish for great tasting and well balanced camp meals.

But don't take our word alone for it. Go ahead. Look at our menus. Try them, and see how easy you can satisfy your campers needs!

BEST EVER BEANS

1 16 ounce can pork and beans
1 12 ounce package of cooked sausage links
1 teaspoon paprika
1 teaspoon chili powder

Place undrained pork and beans in a medium-sized saucepan.
Add sausage links, paprika and chili powder. Stirring
occasionally, heat over campfire or an RV range about 10
minutes until ingredients are piping hot. Or, if desired,
simmer over low heat for about 30 minutes, stirring
occasionally. Serves 4.

*For a hearty touch, serve over fluffy cooked white rice.
Compliment this main dish with our Appetizing Apricots
recipe that follows for a great camp meal.*

APPETIZING APRICOTS

1 12 ounce package of dried apricots
1 cup white cooking sherry
2 teaspoons cinnamon
1/2 teaspoon allspice
dash of nutmeg
dash of cloves

In a medium-sized saucepan, place all of ingredients. Stir.
Stirring occasionally, simmer over a campfire or an RV oven
for about 5 to 10 minutes or until apricots are piping hot .
Serves 4.

QUICK & PRECIOUS PIZZA

1 10¾ ounce can tomato puree
1 teaspoon basil leaves
1/2 teaspoon oregano
dash of pepper
4 English muffins
8 medium sized slices of summer sausage
8 slices Mozzarella cheese

In a bowl, place tomato puree and spices; stir. Cut muffins
crosswise into halves. Spread one or two spoonsful of spiced
tomato puree onto cut sides of muffins. Place a slice of
sausage and cheese on top. Put mini pizza muffins on a
greased or nonstick open container like a cake pan or cookie
sheet. Heat over a medium-hot campfire or in an RV oven
preheated at 375 degrees F. Heat until piping hot and cheese
is melted and bubbly, about 10 to 15 minutes. Serves 4.

*For our hearty tip, serve with a platter of raw broccoli and
cauliflower flowerettes and our following pudding recipe.*

PRETTY 'N TASTY PUDDING

1 8½ ounce can peaches
1 8 ounce can pineapple chunks
1 3 ounce package of instant vanilla pudding
milk

Drain peaches and pineapple chunks well and place in a
serving bowl. Set aside. In a small mixing bowl, stir dry
pudding with milk, using ratio on box directions, until well
mixed. Pour pudding mixture over fruit in the serving bowl.
Let pudding set. Serves 4.

WONDERFUL WIENERS

2 7½ ounce cans prepared biscuits
1 one pound package wieners
mustard
sesame seeds

Open biscuit cans. With clean hands, gently press two
biscuits together to make one large oblong biscuit, making a
total of 5 large biscuits. Spread mustard on one side of
biscuit dough. Put a wiener on top of each mustard-spread
side of oblong biscuits. Wrap biscuit long ends around
wieners and pinch dough edges together. Sprinkle sesame
seeds on top. Place on a greased or nonstick cookie sheet.
Bake in a heated 350 degree F. RV or camp oven for about
12 to 15 minutes or until biscuit dough is done and nicely
browned. Serves 4. *A hearty suggestion: serve with hot
buttered corn on the cob and the following bean salad
recipe.*

BEST BEAN SALAD

1 15 ounce can red kidney beans
1 16 ounce can green beans
1 16 ounce can yellow beans
1/2 cup French or Italian dressing

Drain beans and place in a serving bowl. Add French or
Italian dressing and toss with fork. Chill for at least thirty
minutes in an RV refrigerator or camp cooler before serving.
Serves 6.

BEST BEEF KEBABS

2 pounds beef (round, T-bone or sirloin steak)
1 16 ounce can potatoes
1/2 cup dry red cooking wine
about 2 cups fresh cherry tomatoes
several stalks of celery

Cut beef into cubes. Drain potatoes. Wash tomatoes and celery. Slice celery crosswise into two inch pieces. Thread beef cubes and vegetables on skewers or trimmed green tree sticks. Pour cooking wine over prepared kebabs. Cook over a campfire or in an RV broiler to desired length of cooking time for beef and vegetables. Serves 4. *For the hearty tip, serve with cottage cheese, whole wheat crackers and our following cake.*

CLEVER SPICE CAKE

3 oranges
1 8½ ounce box of spice cake mix
1/2 cup water

Cut a circle around fresh oranges with knife. Peel carefully to get two empty orange cups. In a bowl, prepare cake batter by blending cake mix and water. Pour batter into three orange half cups until each cup is about two-thirds full. Place top orange cups over cake-filled orange cups and secure with toothpicks. Wrap individually in aluminum foil. Bake directly on hot coals or in a 350 degree F. RV oven for about 20 minutes or until cake is done in center. Serves 3. For larger or smaller servings, recipe for cake batter can be doubled or halved to meet campers needs. *Clever and good!*

Chapter 7   It'll Look Like You've Worked!

Want some clever camp meals for your next camp outing that will make your crew think like you've worked all day? Try our delicious food dishes that please every camper from children to grownups. These recipes not only taste great but can be made with a minimum amount of preparation.

LAZY LUNCHEON SPECIAL

1 8 ounce can tomato sauce
2 tablespoons brown sugar
1/4 cup vinegar
1/2 teaspoon Worcestershire sauce
1 tablespoon A-1 steak sauce
1 teaspoon dry mustard
1 teaspoon onion salt
1 tablespoon chili powder
1 one pound package of wieners or
10 wieners

Place all of ingredients, except wieners, in a large frying pan. Stir well. Simmer over hot charcoals or an RV range for about 5 minutes, stirring occasionally. Slice wieners crosswise and place in sauce. Simmer an additional 10 minutes, stirring occasionally. Serve over a bed of hot, fluffy rice. Serves 4. *Menu suggestion: Serve with buttery broccoli, crusty French bread and fresh apples.*

SWEET AND SOUR PORK

1 pound pork tenderloin
1 tablespoon butter or margarine
1 tablespoon soy sauce
2 tablespoons corn starch
1/4 cup pineapple juice
3/4 cup water
1 chicken bouillon cube
1/4 teaspoon horseradish
1 medium onion, diced
1 green pepper, diced
1 can pineapple chunks

Cut pork into one or two inch cubes. Place cut pork in a medium saucepan. Add butter or margarine and soy sauce. Heat over campfire or an RV range, stirring occasionally, until butter is melted and pork is tender.

Mix cornstarch with pineapple juice and water in a small bowl. Add to pork cubes in saucepan. Add bouillon cube. Stir and heat until bouillon cube is dissolved. Add horseradish and stir. Add diced vegetables to pork in sauce and stir. Add drained pineapple chunks. Cook slowly, stirring occasionally, for about 10 minutes. Do not overcook; onion and green pepper should be piping hot but crisp. If mixture gets too thick, add additional water. Serve over a bed of Chinese noodles. Serves 4. *Menu suggestion: Serve with cut orange slices, spinach salad, crisp crackers and butter.*

HEAVENLY GLAZED HAM

1 ½-inch thick slice of ham
1 cup orange juice
1/4 cup brown sugar
1 cup sliced peaches, drained

Cook ham in pan over campfire or an RV range for about 10 minutes on each side. Remove and keep hot by covering in a dish or tin foil. Put orange juice and brown sugar in pan and stir while bringing mixture to a boil. Add peach slices. Stirring occasionally, cook until peach slices are steamy hot. Place glazed peaches on top of ham. Pour remaining orange juice mixture over ham. Serves 4. *Menu suggestion: Serve with baked potatoes, coleslaw, biscuits and vanilla pudding.*

SPECIAL STEAK STRIPS

1 pound round steak
1 teaspoon black pepper
1 tablespoon butter or margarine
1/4 cup Worcestershire sauce
1 cup A-1 steak sauce

Cut round steak into strips and sprinkle black pepper on top. Place peppered steak strips in a frying pan. Add butter or margarine. Stirring occasionally, cook over a campfire or an RV range until butter is melted and steak strips are tender. Mix Worcestershire sauce and A-1 steak sauce in a small bowl. Pour mixture over steak strips and simmer, stirring occasionally, until ingredients are piping hot, about 5 minutes. Serves 4. *Menu suggestion: Serve with hash brown potatoes, cooked carrots, whole wheat bread and fresh pears.*

BEST BARBECUED CHICKEN

1/4 cup tomato ketchup
2 tablespoons brown sugar
juice of 1 lemon
1 tablespoon paprika
1/4 teaspoon black pepper
2 tablespoons A-1 steak sauce
1 teaspoon mustard
1 tablespoon chili powder
dash of garlic salt
dash of onion salt
4 large chicken breasts

Combine all ingredients, except chicken, in a saucepan. Stir.
Stirring occasionally, simmer over campfire or an RV range
until ingredients are well blended.

Dip chicken breasts in sauce. Place barbecue-coated chicken
breasts in a large frying pan lined with aluminum foil. Pour
remaining sauce over chicken. Cover with foil and cook over
hot coals or a 350 degree F. RV oven for about an hour, or
until chicken is nicely done. Serves 4. *Menu suggestion:
Serve with potato salad, buttered peas, cornbread muffins
and fresh apples.*

Unit 4
Recipes For Easy Clean Up

Chapter 8   No Foolin', A Paper Bag Breakfast!

Bag your next camp breakfast. A paper bag breakfast is great
for camping. The all-American bacon and egg breakfast can be
cooked quick and easy in a paper bag. And after this breakfast
is cooked, it can be eaten right out of the bag! That way there's
no messy breakfast clean-up to delay your camping fun.

The beginner as well as the advanced camp cook can prepare a
paper bag breakfast successfully. It's simple. Start by getting a
charcoal fire going.

While the charcoals get hot and turn white, wrap two or three
slices of bacon around a green tree branch stick. Wrap the
bacon in a spiral fashion on the stick. Don't overlap the bacon
edges, so it can cook evenly. Cook the wrapped bacon on the
stick by holding it over the hot charcoals for a few minutes.
Cook until bacon is partially crisp.

Next spread the partially cooked bacon on the bottom of the
paper bag. Use a small bag. Make sure the entire bottom of the
bag is covered with bacon. This is important. If the bag bottom
isn't completely covered with bacon, the bag may catch fire
when held over the hot charcoals later. For a small bag, usually
about three or four bacon slices are sufficient and there's no
need to crumble the bacon.

For the hearty breakfast eater, add a half cup of frozen hash
brown potatoes to the bag. Next break one or two eggs over
the paper bag so they land on top of the potatoes or bacon if you

omit the potatoes. Close the bag shut. Punch a hole, with a knife, about six inches from the top of the bag. Insert the green stick through this hole.

To finish cooking this breakfast, simply hold the bag with the stick over the hot coals. As the bacon finishes cooking in the paper bag, it will automatically grease the bottom of the bag. This is good. The coating of grease prevents the bag from burning. It also keeps the food from sticking to the bag.

It takes about five to ten minutes for the eggs to cook. Extra cooking time is needed if you put the hash brown potatoes in the bag also.

For a special final touch, try this. After the breakfast is cooked, open the bag and place a slice of American cheese on top of the eggs. Close the bag and let the cheese partially melt. This takes about a minute and no extra heating over hot charcoals is required. Simply set the bag at the breakfast table. After the cheese is melted around the edges, roll and tear the bag ends down for eating.

And don't stop there. For a hearty and extra nutritious breakfast, include one of our delicious fruit salads with your bacon and egg recipe. A great compliment to the meal!

BEST BANANAS

1 banana
2 tablespoons apricot jam

Peel and slice banana lengthwise. Spread cut banana insides with apricot jam. Press banana halves back into original position. Slice crosswise for serving. Serves 1.

APPLE APPETIZER SALAD

1 apple
1/4 cup raw cranberries

Wash, core and slice apple. Wash cranberries. Toss ingredients together. Serves 1.

PEACH `N BERRY SALAD

1 fresh peach
1/4 cup fresh blueberries

Peel and slice peach. Arrange peaches in a circling spiral. Heap blueberries on top in center of peach slices. Serves 1.

DELUXE GRAPEFRUIT SALAD

1 grapefruit
1/4 cup raisins
1/4 cup Cherrios

Cut grapefruit in halve. Sprinkle raisins and Cherrios on top of grapefruit halves. Serves 1 or 2.

Chapter 9   Throw Away The Dishes For This Camp Meal!

I hate washing and drying camping dishes. It's miserable to scrub soot covered pots and pans. And when I must watch my family swimming and canoeing in a nearby lake at this same time, it's agony.

The clear, sparkling, blue lake water contrasts with my greasy, gray dishwater. That contrast upset me so much I had to find a way to avoid it.

Since my dishwasher won't fit in the trunk of our car, I solved my problem another way. Now, when my family goes swimming after mealtime, I throw my dishes away and go with them. Maybe that sounds as silly as trying to pack a dishwasher in the trunk of a car. But stop and think about it a minute.

Dishes can be thrown away, if they're disposable! The first thing I pack for camping is a roll of disposable pots and pans, better known as aluminum foil. Aluminum foil is the next thing to magic for a camper. You can store food in it. You can cook food in it. You can even eat from it. It's also compact. A package of foil can slide into the narrowest corner of a box of camping supplies. It's perfect for backpacking trips also. Sheets of foil can be torn off, folded flat and placed in the side pocket of a backpack.

On top of that, aluminum foil isn't expensive. One large roll lasts my family of four for a week's camping trip. I discovered the "heavy-duty" foil lasts even longer. It's higher priced, but it's worth the extra cost. It doesn't have to be doubled in thickness for cooking due to its extra durability.

The use of aluminum foil eliminates the packaging of other items. Pot-holders, steel wool pads, serving bowls, pots and pans can be left home.

Besides aluminum foil, I depend on paper and plastic products to avoid dish-washing. I pack paper plates, cups and napkins. Plastic forks, knives and spoons are also used for my family outings. These products aren't as expensive as they may seem. Often grocery and department stores have sales on these items. Check these sales and buy accordingly.

These disposable products are so easy to use they make camping a joy. When cooking with aluminum foil, I tear off a strip of foil large enough to cover the food I'm preparing plus six or eight extra inches. The extra allowance is for a "tent."

To make the tent, I place the food in middle of the foil, raise the foil in a tent shape and wrap foil ends tightly.

The tent works like a small oven. It allows steam to circulate properly while the food is cooking. It also prevents evaporation of natural food juices. This results in excellent tasting foods high in vitamins.

Numerous dishes can be made with aluminum foil tents. Hot meats, vegetable casseroles and fruit desserts can be cooked with them. Cold salads can be prepared, and served!, in foil tents. (See recipe for tossed salad.)

I use a charcoal fire for foods that require cooking. After wrapping the food, I put the tents directly on the hot coals to cook. This way there's no rack to wash and it reduces cooking time.

Before starting the charcoal fire, I like to line the grill with aluminum foil. Then when clean-up time arrives, I bring the ends of the foil up around the cooled charcoal and toss in a garbage can.

That way when we are camping or backpacking where no garbage cans are available, the disposing of garbage is not a problem. All the paper and plastic products can be burned. I simply add them to the evening camp fire.

Although aluminum foil won't burn, I toss it in the fire anyway. That way the grease and food particles are burned off the foil. Later I pick up the foil and put it in a small box or sack. It's odorless and dry so I can carry it in the car until a garbage can is available. This leaves our campsite clean and unpolluted for the next campers.

The next time you go camping, give yourself a treat. Try the disposable dishes dinner menu below. Then after eating you can have your hands in clear, blue, sparkling lake water instead of greasy, gray dishwater.

HOBO DINNERS

1 potato
1 carrot
1 onion slice
1 hamburger patty
several pats of butter or margarine

For each serving, place a thick hamburger patty in middle of foil.
Peel and quarter potato. Place on hamburger. Peel carrot and
slice crosswise. Place on potato. Put onion slice on top.

Season with salt and pepper to taste. Put several pats of butter
or margarine on meat and vegetables. Wrap foil into a tent.
Cook directly on hot coals for 40 to 50 minutes. Serves 1.

TOSSED SALAD

1 head lettuce, chopped
1 zucchini, sliced
1/2 cup cheese, cubed
dash of seasoned salt
pepper to taste
1/4 cup Italian dressing

Put all ingredients on large piece of foil. Wrap ends of foil
together. Shake until salad ingredients are well moistened with
salad dressing. Untie foil ends and roll part way down. Serve
salad in foil. Serves 4.

FRENCH BREAD

Cut a loaf of French bread in slices part way down, being careful not to cut through the bottom crust. Spread partially-cut slices with butter or margarine. Press slices together to retain the bread's original shape. Wrap in aluminum foil tent. Place beside hot coals. Heat for about 10 minutes or until piping hot.

PRECIOUS PEACH DESSERT

canned or fresh peaches
cream cheese
peanuts

For each serving, place a halved peach in middle of foil. Put a small hunk of cream cheese in peach hole. Sprinkle some peanuts on top. Wrap in foil tent. Place on coals and heat for 5 to 10 minutes or until hot.

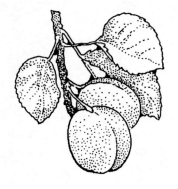

Chapter 10 The Disposable Salad Bowl

Campers and RV'ers love cold crisp salads. And over the years my family and I developed some especially easy ones to prepare. Our secret? These salads require little or no cooking equipment; making clean up super easy! But don't let the easy preparation fool you. These salads taste like you've fussed all day.

Notice some of our salads are served in attractive fruit rinds while others are prepared with the convenience of aluminum foil.

Can't wait to begin? Simply follow our tasty recipes for a bound-to-please dish every camper is sure to enjoy!

FRESH FRUIT AND CREAM SALAD

2 bananas
1 cup fresh peaches
1 cup fresh strawberries
1 cup whipped cream

Peel and slice bananas; remove pit, peel and slice peaches; wash
and hull strawberries. Place prepared fruits on a large sheet of
aluminum foil. Add whipped cream. Fold foil ends together into
a large ball and shake lightly until fruit is covered nicely with
whipped cream. Unfold ends and serve in foil. Serves 4.

SPECIAL SPINACH SALAD

1 large bunch fresh spinach leaves
1 cup orange sections, canned or fresh
1 cup croutons
1/4 cup bacon bits
pepper to taste
1/2 cup French dressing

Wash spinach leaves. Tear or cut spinach into bite sized pieces.
Place spinach on a large sheet of aluminum foil. Add orange
sections. Sprinkle croutons, bacon bits and pepper on salad
ingredients. Add French dressing. Fold foil ends together into a
large ball and shake lightly until ingredients are nicely tossed and
coated with dressing. Unfold ends and serve in foil. Serves 4.

CLEVER COCONUT CARROT SALAD

2 cups carrots, shredded
1/2 cup celery, diced
1/2 cup flaked coconut
1/4 cup orange juice
1 small carton orange yogurt

Wash and shred carrots with a grater and place carrots on a large sheet of aluminum foil. Add diced celery and flaked coconut. In a small mixing bowl, stir orange juice and yogurt together. Pour over salad ingredients placed on aluminum foil. Fold foil ends together into a large ball and shake lightly until fruit is covered with dressing. Unfold foil ends and serve in foil. Serves 4.

DELICIOUS PORK & BEAN SALAD

1 can pork 'n beans
1/2 green pepper, diced
1/2 onion, diced
1/2 cup ranch salad dressing

Drain pork 'n beans and place drained beans on a large sheet of aluminum foil. Add diced pepper, onion and salad dressing. Fold foil ends together and shake until ingredients are nicely covered with salad dressing. Unfold foil ends and serve in foil. Serves 4.

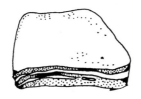

PRECIOUS PEA SALAD

1 can peas, drained
1 cup cheddar cheese, cubed
1 tomato, diced
1/4 teaspoon onion salt
dash of garlic salt
pepper to taste
1/2 cup buttermilk salad dressing

Place drained peas on a large sheet of aluminum foil. Add cheese and tomato, then sprinkle with onion salt, garlic salt and pepper. Add buttermilk salad dressing. Fold foil ends together and shake until ingredients are nicely moistened with salad dressing. Unfold foil ends and serve in foil. Serves 4.

BEST BROCCOLI SALAD

1 bunch fresh broccoli
2 hard-cooked eggs, peeled and sliced
1 can pitted black olives, drained
1/2 cup Russian dressing

Wash broccoli, cut into bite-sized pieces and place on a large sheet of aluminum foil. Add prepared egg slices and drained olives. Top with Russian dressing. Fold foil ends together into a large ball and shake until ingredients are nicely moistened with salad dressing. Unfold foil ends and serve in foil. Serves 4 to 6.

Unit 5
Recipes For Fall/Winter

Chapter 11   Hot & Hearty Meals For Winter Camping

Burrrrrr. Nothing raises a camper's appetite like the winter outdoors. The camp meals featured here were developed especially for winter campers. All the meals feature hot, hearty and nutritious foods that are simple to prepare.

The preparation simplicity of these meals is a big plus. Winter campers don't like to peel and chop potatoes and other vegetables. Nor do they like to mess with a lot of cooking utensils.

And who can blame them? Winter camping should be enjoyed by hunting, snowmobiling and hiking!

HAM HAVEN

1 thick center slice ham, cooked
1 10¾ ounce can string beans
1 10¾ ounce can mushroom soup
1 teaspoon dry mustard

Place ham slice in a large frying pan. Brown bottom side of ham over campfire or an RV range and turn ham slice. Drain string beans and place on top of ham. Pour mushroom soup on top of beans and ham. Sprinkle dry mustard on top. Heat until all ingredients are piping hot. Serves 4. *Menu suggestion: Baked potatoes, corn and crescent dinner rolls.*

SPAM DELUXE

1 12 ounce can Spam
1 32 ounce package of frozen hash browns
6 eggs
salt and pepper

Slice Spam and place in a large frying pan. Cook over campfire or an RV range until lightly browned on both sides. Push Spam to the edges and place the frozen hash brown potatoes in the middle. Fry potatoes, turning occasionally, until they are nicely browned. Crack eggs and place on top of fried potatoes. Salt and pepper to taste. Place lid on pan and cook until eggs are just set. Serves 4. *Menu Suggestion: Buttered peas, oranges and biscuits.*

SAUSAGE SPECIAL

1 10¾ ounce can lima beans
1 12 ounce package cooked sausage links
1 10¾ ounce can cheese soup
1 tablespoon chili powder

Drain lima beans and place in a large saucepan. Add sausage links, cheese soup and chili powder. Lightly toss with rubber spatula or wooden spoon until all ingredients are coated with cheese soup and chili powder. Heat until piping hot. Serves 4. *Menu Suggestion: Buttered egg noodles, grapefruit halves and French bread.*

CHICKEN-VEGETABLE DELIGHT

1 6½ ounce can boned and cooked chicken
1 10¾ ounce can carrots
1 10¾ ounce can peas
1 10¾ ounce can chili soup
3/4 cup water
1 8½ ounce can onion rings

Drain chicken, carrots and peas and place in a large saucepan. Add chili soup and water. Lightly toss with rubber spatula or wooden spoon until all ingredients are coated with chili soup mixture. Heat over campfire or RV range until piping hot. Just before serving, add onion rings. Serves 4. *Menu Suggestion: Mashed potatoes, canned peaches and brown-raisin bread.*

WIENER CASSEROLE

1 10½ ounce can small whole potatoes
1 10¾ ounce can cream of celery soup
6 wieners, sliced crosswise
1 10¾ ounce can corn

Drain potatoes and place in a large saucepan. Add cream of celery soup and sliced wieners. Drain corn and add. Lightly toss with rubber spatula or wooden spoon until ingredients are nicely coated with soup. Cook over campfire or RV range until piping hot. Serves 4. *Menu suggestion: Baked beans, canned pears and buttered toast.*

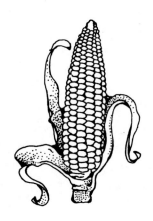

Chapter 12   **Warm Your Winter Days With These Tasty Stews**

Sure, a steaming hot bowl of stew tastes great on a cold, wintry day. But who has time to make it at camp?

Hold it! With our recipes, you can make a camp stew in a snap. The recipes take about 20 minutes to complete, 5 minutes for preparation and 15 minutes for cooking time. These delicious stews will taste like you've fussed all day, though. Just the right combination of ingredients and seasonings creates a great taste every time! And if you'd rather leave your stew simmering for several hours for an extra toasty warm campsite, that's fine too.

CLEVER CHICKEN AND CARROT STEW

2 2½ ounce cans boned chicken in broth
1 one pound can carrots, undrained
2 10¾ ounce cans mushroom soup
3 cups milk
1/2 cup celery, diced
1/2 cup mushrooms, sliced
1 chicken bouillon cube

Place all of ingredients in a 5 quart saucepan. Stirring frequently, simmer over campfire or RV range for about 15 minutes or until bouillon cube is dissolved and ingredients are piping hot. Serves 4 to 6.

BEST BEEF STEW

2 10 ounce cans beef in broth
1 beef bouillon cube
2 cups water
1 15 ounce can green lima beans, undrained
1½ cups cooked rice
1/8 teaspoon black pepper
1 teaspoon basil leaves
1 tablespoon butter or margarine

Place all of ingredients in a 5 quart saucepan. Stirring frequently, simmer over campfire or RV range for about 15 minutes or until bouillon cube is dissolved and ingredients are piping hot. Serves 4 to 6.

WONDERFUL WIENER STEW

1 12 ounce package wide noodles
1 one-pound package wieners, sliced
2 tablespoons margarine or butter
1 2½ ounce can mushrooms, undrained
1 10¾ ounce can cream of celery soup
1 10¾ ounce can cream of mushroom soup
3 cups milk

Cook noodles according to package directions; drain and set aside. Place sliced wieners in pan with margarine or butter. Cook over campfire hot charcoals or RV range until lightly browned. Add mushrooms with liquid and stir and cook for about a minute. In a bowl, mix soups and milk together; pour mixture in pan with wieners and undrained mushrooms. Stir. Add cooked noodles. Stirring occasionally, cook over low heat for about 20 to 30 minutes. Serves 4 to 6.

CLEVER CHILI STEW

3 tablespoons chili powder
1 pound hamburger
1 cup rice, cooked
2 15 ounce cans red kidney beans, undrained
2 10¾ ounce cans tomato puree
3 cups tomato juice
1/4 teaspoon garlic salt

Mix chili powder into hamburger. Fry seasoned meat in pan over campfire hot coals or RV range until browned. Add cooked rice with rest of ingredients. Stir. Simmer for 20 to 30 minutes, stirring occasionally. Serves 4 to 6.

HEARTY HAM STEW

1/4 cup margarine or butter
1/4 cup flour
3 cups milk
6 cups potatoes, peeled and sliced
1/4 cup onion, diced
2 chicken bouillon cubes
3 cups water
2 cups ham, cooked and cubed
1   15¼ ounce can corn, undrained

Make cream sauce, using the first three ingredients. To do this, melt margarine or butter in a pan over campfire hot charcoals or RV range. Blend in flour. Add milk, a little at a time to prevent lumping. Cook over low heat, stirring constantly, until sauce is thickened. Set aside for use later. Place prepared potatoes, onion, chicken bouillon cubes and water in a large saucepan. Cook, over medium to low heat, until potatoes and onions are tender and bouillon cubes dissolved. Add cream sauce, ham and corn. Stir. Heat for 10 to 15 minutes, stirring occasionally. Serves 4 to 6.

CRAFTY CHICKEN STEW

2 tablespoons margarine or butter
2 cups chicken, cooked and cubed
1 onion, peeled and quartered
1 teaspoon Worcestershire sauce
2 10¾ ounce cans cheese soup
4 cups milk
2 potatoes, sliced and cooked
2 cups rice, cooked
1 teaspoon seasoned salt
1/3 cup French dressing

Melt margarine or butter in large pan over campfire or RV range. Add chicken, onion and Worcestershire sauce and cook for a minute or until onion is tender. Add cheese soup and milk and stir. Add cooked potatoes, cooked rice, pepper, seasoned salt and French dressing. Stir. Cook over low heat, stirring occasionally, for about 20 to 30 minutes. Serves 4 to 6.

SPECIAL SHRIMP STEW

2 10¾ ounce cans cream of broccoli or celery soup
4 cups milk
1/2 cup cheddar cheese, grated
1 12 ounce package devained and precooked shrimp
2 cups shell macaroni, cooked

Place first three ingredients in large pan and stir. Heat over campfire or RV range until cheese is melted. Add shrimp, cooked macaroni. Stir. Heat, stirring occasionally, for 20 to 30 minutes until flavors are well blended. Serves 4 to 6.

Chapter 13 Hot & Hearty Camp Desserts

Look at what we've got. Delicious hot and hearty camp desserts that can be prepared in minutes. No longer do you have to slave over the stove to come up with a dessert winter campers will enjoy.

Take a look at our recipes. They're so easy to prepare! Note none of the recipes call for expensive ingredients or messy and time consuming preparation methods.

Not at all. Developed especially for winter camping, our desserts are prepared using simple procedures and taste great. A great deal for campers as well as the camp chef!

BEST BANANA & ORANGE DELUXE

4 bananas
2 oranges
2 tablespoons minced orange rind
1 tablespoon margarine
1 tablespoon soy sauce

Peel bananas; slice crosswise. Peel oranges; pull sections apart.
In a skillet, melt margarine over low heat using an RV range or a
camp fire. Add soy sauce. Stir. Add peeled and sliced bananas,
orange sections and minced orange rind. Cook over medium
heat, stirring occasionally, until fruits are piping hot for serving.
Enjoy! Serves 4 to 6.

APPETIZING APPLE DESSERT

4 large apples
2 tablespoons margarine or butter
2 tablespoons apple juice or water
1 teaspoon cinnamon
1/8 teaspoon nutmeg
dash of cloves
1/4 cup slivered almonds

Wash apples; core and dice, leaving on fruit skin if desired.
In a skillet, melt margarine or butter over low heat using an RV
range or a camp fire. Add apple juice or water, cinnamon,
nutmeg and cloves. Stir. Add almonds and diced apples. Cook
over medium heat, stirring occasionally, until apples are just
tender and piping hot. Delicious! Serves 4.

BEST BREAD PUDDING

3 slices of dried bread
2 cups milk
1/4 cup sugar
3 eggs
1 tablespoon vanilla
1 cup chocolate chips

Tear bread into bite-size pieces. In a skillet, heat milk until hot, stirring occasionally to prevent burning, using an RV range or a camp fire. Place torn bread in milk and remove from heat, letting bread absorb milk. Meanwhile, in a small bowl, place sugar, eggs and vanilla and stir. Place bread and milk back on heat and pour mixed egg mixture over bread. Cook, stirring occasionally, until egg mixture is set. Add chocolate chips and stir gently until chips are partially melted. Serve plain or with whipped cream. Serves 4.

CLEVER CHERRY DELIGHT

1 21 ounce can cherry pie filling
1 8½ ounce box white cake mix
1 stick of margarine
1 cup coconut
1 cup walnuts

Place cherry filling in a 7x11 cake pan. Using a spatula, spread cherry filling in pan. Sprinkle dry cake mix, coconut and walnuts over cherries. Melt margarine and drizzle over mixture. Bake in a camp or RV oven at 350 degree F. for about 15 or 20 minutes. Cut into squares and serve. Serves about 8.

OH SO DELICIOUS APPLESAUCE

1 16 ounce can applesauce
1 small package or about 1/2 cup cinnamon candies

In a saucepan, place applesauce and cinnamon candies. Cook, over low heat, using an RV range or a camp fire. Stir occasionally to prevent burning. Cook until applesauce is piping hot and cinnamon candies are partially or fully melted, depending on taste. Stir and serve. Best ever! Serves about 4.

GREAT GINGERBREAD

1 16 ounce can of peaches
1 6 ounce jar maraschino cherries
1 9 ounce box of gingerbread mix

Drain peaches and cherries. Prepare gingerbread according to package directions. Spread drained peaches and cherries in a 7x11 baking cake pan. Pour gingerbread mixture over fruit. Bake according to gingerbread package directions. Serves about 8.

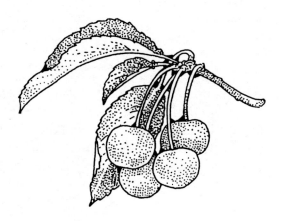

Chapter 14 **Winter Delight: Snow Ice Cream!**

Snow ice cream is a treat for campers. And no need to bring an ice cream freezer, salt and ice for the camp trip either. With snow ice cream, everything's left to mother nature.

When making snow ice cream, the main thing is to make sure the snow is clean and even this isn't as hard to do as it may sound. Simply brush the top layers of snow, about one inch deep, aside with a spatula or some other utensil. Remember, top-layered snow is clean only immediately after snowfall. It doesn't take long for dirt and other unclean air particles to settle on the surface. After brushing the top snow aside, scoop out as much snow as needed from middle layers. Of course, the bottom layers of snow need to be avoided for snow ice cream. These layers are easy to identify since they're tan or brown from the dirt close beneath the snow.

Surprisingly, it doesn't take a deep snowfall to make snow ice cream. I've made snow ice cream with only four to six inches of snow on the ground. As long as the middle layers of snow are clean white, you're in business. Snow ice cream can be made to perfection. Ice cream too thick? Add some cream or milk. Ice cream too thin? Add some snow.

Snow ice creams should be served immediately after preparation, since they can't be stored successfully in a freezer or cooler. But that's no problem either. Our featured recipes can be halved or doubled to meet individual camp sized needs.

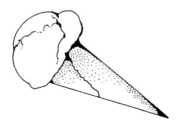

OLD FASHIONED VANILLA ICE CREAM

1/3 cup sugar
1/2 cup cream
1/2 cup milk
2 teaspoons vanilla
5 cups snow

Mix cream and sugar together in a large bowl. Stir until mixed.
Add milk, vanilla and snow. Stir until ingredients are well mixed
and mixture is thick. Serves 4 to 6.

ORANGE ICE CREAM

1/2 cup frozen orange juice concentrate
1/4 cup sugar
1/2 cup cream
4 cups snow

Mix orange juice concentrate, sugar and cream together in a
large bowl. Stir until mixed. Add snow. Stir until all
ingredients are well mixed. Variation: Substitute lemon or lime
frozen concentrate for orange. Serves 4 to 6.

BEST BUTTER BRICKEL

1/2 cup brown sugar
1/4 cup regulated sugar
1/2 cup cream
1/2 cup milk
1½ teaspoons butter flavoring
1 teaspoon vanilla flavoring
5 cups snow
1/4 cup butter baking chips

Mix brown sugar, regulated sugar, cream and milk together in a large bowl. Stir until mixed. Add flavorings, snow and butter chips. Stir until all ingredients are well mixed. Serves 4 to 6.

PISTACHIO ICE CREAM

1/3 cup pistachio instant pudding mix
1/2 cup half & half cream
1/4 cup milk
4 cups snow

Mix pistachio pudding mix with half & half cream in a large bowl. Stir until mixed. Add milk and snow. Stir until all ingredients are well mixed. Serves 4 to 6.

BLUEBERRY FROZEN YOGURT

1 small carton blueberry yogurt
1/2 cup half & half cream
5 cups snow

Mix blueberry yogurt and half & half cream together in a large bowl. Stir until mixed. Add snow. Stir until all ingredients are mixed. Variation: Substitute raspberry or strawberry yogurt for blueberry. Serves 4 to 6.

PEPPERMINT ICE CREAM

1/4 cup sugar
1/2 cup cream
1/4 cup hard peppermint candy, crushed
1 teaspoon peppermint flavoring
3/4 cup milk
5 cups snow

Mix sugar and cream together in a large bowl. Stir until mixed. Crush hard peppermint candy and add to sugar and cream mixture. Add milk, peppermint flavoring and snow. Stir until all ingredients are mixed. (Peppermint candies, even though crushed, will remain hard for a nice and rich crunch ice cream). Serves 4 to 6.

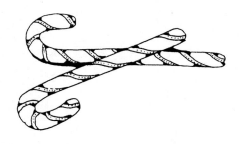

PINEAPPLE ICE CREAM

1/4 cup sugar
1/2 cup cream
1/4 cup milk
1/4 cup pineapple juice
1 teaspoon vanilla
5 cups snow
1/2 cup crushed pineapple, well drained

Mix sugar and cream together in a large bowl. Stir until mixed.
Add milk, pineapple juice, vanilla and snow. Stir until all
ingredients are well mixed. With a rubber spatula, gently fold
the crushed pineapple into the ice-cream mixture. Serves 4 to 6.

CHERRY SWIRL

1/4 cup sugar
1 cup cream
2 teaspoons vanilla
5 cups snow
1/3 cup cherry flavored ready made pie filling

Mix sugar and cream together in a large bowl. Stir until mixed.
Add vanilla and snow. Stir until all ingredients are well mixed.
With a rubber spatula, swirl the cherry pie filling gently into the
ice-cream mixture. Variation: Substitute blueberry or peach pie
filling for cherry. Serves 4 to 6.

Unit 6
Recipes For Spring and Summer

Chapter 15   Cold And Clever Camp Meals

Sure, you like to camp. But you don't cherish the idea of pulling into a campsite at dinner time with a hungry family. Who would?

But with our recipes you can eat only minutes after you arrive at your destination! Featuring menus that are served cold, our recipes can be prepared the day before you leave home.

Simply pack one of these prepared menu dishes in your cooler for your next summer camp trip. A real treat!

BEST BEAN SALAD

1 large tomato, diced
1 avocado, peeled and sliced
1 medium onion, peeled and diced
1 28 ounce can of pork and beans
1/2 cup salad dressing

Wash and dice tomato. Peel and slice avocado. Peel and slice onion. Place prepared tomato, avocado and onion in a bowl with pork and beans and salad dressing. Mix gently with rubber spatula until all ingredients are nicely moistened with salad dressing. Keep in refrigerator or cooler. (Keeps well for about 2 or 3 days.) Serves 4. *Suggestion: Serve with cheese sandwiches and a bowl of fresh fruit.*

HEARTY HAM SANDWICHES

1 27 ounce can sauerkraut
1 teaspoon celery seed (optional)
2 apples, diced
2 cups shaved and cooked ham slices
mustard
sandwich rolls

Drain sauerkraut. Add celery seed to kraut in a mixing bowl. Wash, core and dice apples. Add diced apples to sauerkraut mixture. Toss with a fork. Open sandwich rolls and, with a dull knife, spread mustard on insides. Place a hearty helping of sauerkraut mixture in mustard-spread sandwich rolls. Add a hearty heaping of shaved ham slices. Close sandwich rolls and place in refrigerator or keep in cooler. (Keeps well for 1 or 2 days.) Serves 4. *Suggestion: Serve with potato chips, carrot strips and fresh pineapple.*

Rich Rice Salad

1 cup rice
2 10¾ ounce cans tomato puree
6 wieners, sliced crosswise
1/4 cup onion, peeled and diced
1/4 cup green pepper, washed, discard seeds and membrane and dice

Prepare rice according to package directions. Drain rice and add tomato puree and wieners and toss. Add prepared vegetables and mix gently with a rubber spatula. Keep in refrigerator or cooler. (Keeps well for 1 or 2 days.) Serves 4. *Suggestion: Serve with pickled cauliflower and apples.*

Delicious Dinner Salad

4 cups cabbage, shredded
1 cup cottage cheese
5 hard cooked eggs, sliced
2 tablespoons vinegar
1/4 teaspoon dry mustard
1/3 cup buttermilk
1 teaspoon pepper

Wash and shred cabbage. Add cottage cheese and eggs. Mix vinegar, dry mustard, buttermilk and pepper together. Pour over cabbage mixture and toss with a fork. Keep in refrigerator or cooler. (Keeps well for 1 or 2 days.) At campsite, serve over a fresh bed of lettuce. Serves 4. *Suggestion: Serve with sliced tomatoes, cold meats, biscuits and butter and bananas.*

MAIN DISH SALAD

1   7 ounce package shell macaroni
1   7 ounce can tuna
1 cup celery, diced
1 cup ripe olives
1 cup cheddar cheese, cubed
1/2 cup mayonnaise

Cook macaroni according to package directions. Drain tuna and add to cooled, cooked macaroni. Wash and dice celery; add to tuna and macaroni. Drain and add olives. Cut cheese into cubes and add with mayonnaise to tuna mixture. Stir gently with a rubber spatula until all ingredients are nicely moistened with mayonnaise. Keep in refrigerator or cooler. (Keeps well for 2 or 3 days.) Serves 4. *Menu suggestion: Serve with a vegetable relish tray, bread and butter and fresh peaches.*

CLEVER CHICKEN

4 chicken breasts, cooked
2 tomatoes, diced
1/2 cup green olives, drained
1/2 cup Thousand Island dressing
1 teaspoon pepper
1 cup potato chips, crushed

Remove cooked chicken from bones. Remove skin and discard
with bones. Dice cooked chicken. Wash and dice tomatoes;
.drain olives. Place prepared chicken, tomatoes and olives in a
mixing bowl. Add Thousand Island dressing and pepper. Stir
with fork until ingredients are well coated with dressing. At
campsite, simply add fresh potato chips to chicken mixture and
toss lightly with fork. Spread prepared chicken mixture on
French bread rolls. (The chicken mixture, without potato chips,
keeps in refrigerator or cooler for 1 or 2 days.) Serves 4. *Menu
suggestion: Serve with cold pea salad and hard boiled eggs.*

Chapter 16   Cold, Crisp And Clever Vegetables For Camp

Don't hesitate to try these cold, crisp and clever vegetable dishes for a tasty camp snack or as a delicious dish for part of the camp meal. We've included serving sizes for both.

Campers, including children, enjoy these vegetables, which are rich in vitamins. And so does the camp chef. These recipes not only taste great; they're simple to make, too. But don't take our word for it. On your next camp-out, try them for yourself.

Note: All meal size recipes serves four people and snack size serves one person.

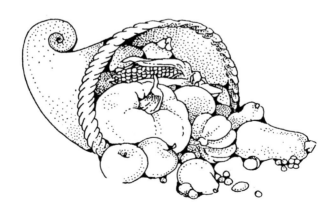

TASTY TOMATOES

Ingredients	Meal	Snack
fresh tomatoes	4	1
grated cheddar	1/2 cup	1/4 cup
pepper	to taste	dash
garlic salt	to taste	dash

Wash tomatoes and slice off stems. Cut tomatoes into four partial sections, leaving the bottom of the vegetable uncut. Gently pull the sections open; place grated cheese in tomato center. Sprinkle with pepper and garlic salt to desired taste.

Snack: Eat as a finger food or place in a small bowl.
Meal: Place tomatoes on a fresh bed of washed spinach leaves.

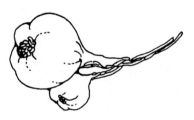

BEST BROCCOLI

Ingredient	Meal	Snack
broccoli, fresh	2 cups	1/2 cup
cherry tomatoes	1 cup	1/4 cup
Velveta cheese	1 cup	1/4 cup
blue cheese dressing	1 cup	none

Cut off flowerettes from fresh broccoli; wash flowerettes and cherry tomatoes. Cut cheese into cubes.

Snack: Place washed vegetables with cheese cubes in a paper cup and eat as a finger food snack.
Meal: Place washed vegetables with cheese cubes in a serving bowl. Pour blue cheese dressing on top and eat with forks.

CLEVER CUCUMBERS

Ingredients	Meal	Snack
cucumbers	4	1
cream cheese	1 cup	1/4 cup
parsley	1 tablespoon	1/2 tsp.
oregano	1/4 teaspoon	dash
black olives		

Peel cucumber and cut in half lengthwise. Remove center seeds and discard. In a small mixing bowl, place cream cheese, parsley and oregano. Stir until spices are well mixed with cream cheese and spoon on top of cucumbers.

Snack: Place several black olives on top of cream cheese and eat as a finger food.
Meal: Place stuffed cucumbers on a tray garnished with black olives and fresh parsley.

CRAFTY CAULIFLOWER

Ingredients	Meal	Snack
fresh cauliflower	3 cups	1 cup
sliced celery	2/3 cup	1/4 cup
sliced onion	2/3 cup	1/4 cup
Thousand Island dressing	1 cup	1/4 cup
carrot curls	a few	none

Cut flowerettes from cauliflower. Wash flowerettes and set aside. Wash and slice celery and onion. Place prepared vegetables in a bowl. Add Thousand Island dressing. Toss with fork until ingredients are moistened with dressing.

Snack: Place in a small snack bowl and eat with fork.
Meal: Place in a serving bowl garnished with carrot curls.

ZESTY ZUCCHINI AND CARROTS

Ingredients	Meal	Snack
zucchini	2 cups	1/2 cup
carrots	2 cups	1/2 cup
pepper	2 teaspoons	1 tsp.
basil leaves	1 teaspoon	1/2 tsp.
wine & oil dressing	1 cup	1/4 cup

Wash and slice zucchini; wash and slice carrots. Place zucchini and carrots in a bowl. Add pepper, basil leaves and wine and oil dressing. Toss gently with a fork until vegetables are nicely moistened with dressing.

Snack: Using a fork, eat in a snack bowl.
Meal: Place prepared dish in a serving bowl lined with a bed of washed fresh lettuce leaves.

LOVELY CELERY

Ingredients	Meal	Snack
celery	6 to 8 sticks	1 stick
Stuffing mix		
catsup	1/4 cup	2 tablespoons
chili powder	1 teaspoon	1/2 teaspoon
cottage cheese	1 cup	1/4 cup

Wash celery and set aside. In a small mixing bowl, place catsup, chili powder and cottage cheese; stir with a spoon until spices are well blended with cottage cheese. Fill washed celery cavities with prepared stuffing mix.

Snack: Eat as a finger food.
Meal: Place celery on tray with olives in center for garnish.

GREAT GREEN PEPPER

Ingredients	Meal	Snack
green peppers	4	1
raisins	1 cup	1/4 cup
fresh pineapple	1 cup	1/4 cup
fresh apples	2	1/2
cinnamon	1 teaspoon	1/4 teaspoon

Remove seeds and inside membrane from green peppers and discard. Wash green peppers. In a small mixing bowl, place raisins and pineapple. Wash, core and slice apples into bite-sized pieces; add to raisins and pineapple. Add cinnamon. Toss with a fork. Fill prepared green peppers with fruit stuffing.

Snack: Eat as a finger food.
Meal: Set prepared green peppers on a serving tray garnished with orange slices.

APPETIZING ASPARAGUS

Ingredients	Meal	Snack
fresh asparagus sticks	about 20	6
Dip mix		
mustard, mild or hot	1/2 cup	1/4 cup
sour cream	1/2 cup	1/4 cup
fresh dill	3/4 teaspoon	1/4 teaspoon
horseradish, optional	1/8 teaspoon	1/8 teaspoon

Wash asparagus and set aside. In a small mixing bowl, place rest of ingredients. Stir with a spoon until well mixed.

Snack or meal serving: Place dip in a small serving dish for use with asparagus sticks for a snack or meal.

Chapter 17 Main Dish Salads for Easy Camp Dinners

Nothing's more refreshing than a hearty cold salad for a main dish camp meal on a hot summer day. And our salads are made with little or no cooking equipment for a hassle-free clean-up.

Go ahead and relax with these main dish salads. Serve with a bowl of fresh fruit and a cold beverage for a complete camp meal.

CHICKEN SALAD

2 large apples
1 avocado
1/2 cup raisins
1/2 cup walnuts
1/2 cup coconut
2 cups chicken, cooked and cubed
1 cup Bleu Cheese or Thousand Island salad dressing

Wash, core and dice apples. Peel, pit and slice avocado. Place
prepared apples and avocado on a large sheet of aluminum foil.
Add raisins, walnuts, coconut and cooked chicken cubes on foil
sheet. Pour salad dressing of your choice over prepared salad
ingredients. Squeeze foil ends shut and shake for a few seconds
until ingredients are nicely tossed and covered with dressing.
Serves 4.

CABBAGE AND HAM SALAD

1 small head of cabbage, grated
2 cups cold ham, cooked and cubed
1/4 cup green pepper, diced
1/4 cup onion, diced
1 cup cheddar cheese, cubed
1 cup coleslaw dressing

Cook ham. Wash, core and grate cabbage. Place on a large
sheet of aluminum foil. Place prepared ham, diced green pepper,
diced onion and cubed cheese on foil with grated cabbage. Pour
coleslaw dressing over prepared salad ingredients. Squeeze foil
ends into a large ball and shake for a few seconds until
ingredients are nicely tossed and covered with dressing. Unfold
foil ends and serve in foil. Serves 4.

CRAB SALAD IN ORANGE CUPS

4 orange rind shells
2 cups orange segments, diced
1 6 ounce can crab meat
1/2 cup celery, sliced thin
1/2 cup slivered almonds
1 cup Ranch salad dressing

Make the orange rind shells by cutting the rind crosswise, being
careful to not cut into the fruit itself. With clean hands, poke
fingertips into rind shell until it comes off of the orange. Set
orange shells aside. Tear oranges into segments and place into a
mixing bowl. Add crab meat, celery, almonds and dressing.
Toss with fork until ingredients are coated with dressing. Spoon
mixture into orange rind shells. Serves 4.

Tasty Tuna And Pea Salad

1 6 ounce can tuna
1 12 ounce can peas
1 6 ounce can pitted black olives
1/2 cup grated carrots
dash of pepper
1 cup mayonnaise

Drain tuna, peas and olives. Place drained ingredients on a large
sheet of aluminum foil. Peel and grate carrots. Place on top of
other ingredients. Add pepper. Place mayonnaise on top of
ingredients. Squeeze foil ends shut and shake until ingredients
are covered with mayonnaise. Serves 4.

Chapter 18 **July 4th Burgers, Hot Dogs & Pies**

Put pizazz into your hamburger and hot dog camp meals to treat
your campers this 4th of July. Our recipes are bound to give
your 4th of July celebration this year a real lift! In just minutes,
you can make a luscious hamburger or hot dog camp meal your
camp family will love.

Also, keep the patriotic spirit throughout your 4th of July camp
celebration this year by preparing our mouth-watering pies,
featuring red, white and blue colors. Any of the pies can be
made ahead of time and stored in the freezer. In fact, a couple
of the pies are served frozen for a real cool treat! And our
Never Fail Pie Crust recipe is one you can't afford to be without.
It turns out scrumptious every time!

SPECIAL AND SPICY HAMBURGERS

2 pounds hamburger
1/2 cup green pepper, diced
1/2 cup onion, diced
1 tablespoon horseradish
1 teaspoon dry mustard

Mix ingredients together. Shape into 8 patties and cook, in a frying pan, over campfire for 8 to 10 minutes or until browned on both sides. Serve in hamburger buns. Serves 8.

CHEESEBURGERS

2 pounds hamburger
1 cup cheddar cheese, shredded
2 tablespoons Worcestershire sauce

Mix ingredients together. Shape into 8 patties and cook, in a frying pan, over campfire for 8 to 10 minutes or until browned on both sides. Serve in hamburger buns. Serves 8.

ZESTY ONION HAMBURGERS

2 pounds hamburger
one 1½ ounce package of dry onion soup mix

Mix ingredients together. Shape into 8 patties and cook, in a frying pan, over campfire for 8 to 10 minutes or until browned on both sides. Serve in hamburger buns. Serves 8.

HAWAIIAN HAMBURGERS

2 pounds hamburger
1/4 cup soy sauce
1/4 teaspoon ground ginger

Mix ingredients together. Shape into 8 patties and cook, in a frying pan, over campfire for 8 to 10 minutes or until browned on both sides. Serve in hamburger buns. Serves 8.

BEST BARBECUE HAMBURGERS

2 pounds hamburger
1/2 cup tomato sauce
2 tablespoons chili powder
1 teaspoon paprika
1 teaspoon pepper

Mix ingredients together. Shape into 8 patties and cook, in a frying pan, over campfire for 8 to 10 minutes or until browned on both sides. Serves 8.

PERFECT PARTY HAMBURGERS

1½ pounds hamburger
1 cup corn flakes, crushed
1 cup catsup
1 egg, well beaten

Mix ingredients together. Shape into 8 patties and cook, in a frying pan, over campfire for 8 to 10 minutes or until browned on both sides. Serve in hamburger buns. Serves 8.

BEST BEAN HOT DOGS

1 package of 10 wieners
1 15 ounce can pork 'n beans, drained
1 teaspoon barbecue seasoning spice

Partially cut wieners lengthwise. Mix drained pork 'n beans with barbecue seasoning spice. Place spiced beans in cut wiener slits. Cook in a frying pan over an RV range or campfire for about 5 minutes or until wieners and beans are piping hot. Serve in hot dog buns. Serves 10.

HAWAIIAN HOT DOGS

1 package of 10 wieners
1 8 ounce can pineapple, crushed and drained
1 cup small marshmallows
nutmeg

Partially cut wieners lengthwise. Place prepared pineapple and marshmallows in cut wiener slits. Sprinkle nutmeg on top. Cook in a frying pan over campfire until marshmallows are hot and bubbly. Serve in hot dog buns. Serves 10.

TANGY HOT DOGS

1 package of 10 wieners
French salad dressing

Coat wieners with dressing. Using a stick, cook wieners over a campfire until piping hot. Serve in hot dog buns. Serves 10.

FANCY HOT DOGS

1 package of 10 wieners
1 7 ounce can sauerkraut, drained
1 3 ounce can pimento-stuffed green olives
10 long thin cheese slices

Partially cut wieners lengthwise. Place prepared sauerkraut, olives and cheese slices in wiener slits. Cook, covered, in a frying pan over an RV range or campfire for 2 or 3 minutes or until cheese is melted and piping hot. Serves 12.

SPECIAL STRAWBERRY PIE

1   12 ounce package frozen strawberries
1   8 ounce carton sour cream
2 cups whipped cream (already whipped)

Thaw strawberries; don't drain. In a bowl, place cream cheese and sour cream and stir until creamed together.

Using a rubber spatula, fold in strawberries with juice and whipped cream. Pour in baked single pie crust (using our special no-fail crust recipe on the next page or a prepared graham cracker crust.) Freeze and serve frozen. Garnish with a couple fresh strawberries and a dab of whipped cream on each pie piece, if desired. Serves 6 to 8 pie pieces.

BEST BLUEBERRY PIE

3 cups fresh blueberries
1 tablespoon lemon juice
1 cup sugar
1/4 cup flour
2 tablespoons butter or margarine

Wash berries. Sprinkle lemon juice over washed berries. Place prepared berries in a pie crust, using the recipe on the next page.

In a large mixing bowl, place sugar and flour. Stir. Sprinkle mixture over berries in pie crust. Place thin pats of margarine or butter over ingredients. Add top pie crust. Bake in a 350 degree F. RV or home oven for about 45 minutes or until berries are nicely tender. If making at home, store in freezer until planned camp trip. Serves 6 to 8 pie slices.

FAVORITE NEVER FAIL PIE CRUST

3 cups flour
1 teaspoon cream of tartar
1¼ cups shortening
1 egg
1/4 cup water
1 tablespoon vinegar

In a large mixing bowl, place flour and cream of tartar. Stir with a fork. Add shortening. Cut shortening into dry ingredients using a pastry blender or a dull knife.

In a small mixing bowl, place egg, water and vinegar. Stir with a fork until well mixed and frothy. Add to pastry ingredients in large bowl. Stir gently with a fork until ingredients are well mixed. Place dough mixture onto a lightly floured surface and roll with rolling pin. Provides enough mixture for top and bottom pie crusts.

Unit 7   Recipes For Bread Products

Chapter 19   Tasty Camp Biscuits

Homemade biscuits hot from the oven always taste good and our biscuits are especially tasty when baked on a stick over a campfire. Take a look at our simple no fuss cooking method. A paper sack and stick are the only cooking utensils needed. The ingredients are simply tossed in a paper sack and stirred with a stick. Then a dab of the biscuit dough is twisted on a stick and baked over a campfire.

Recipe directions are the same for every biscuit recipe. Only the ingredients vary.

Directions For Campfire Biscuits:

Put the dry ingredients in a heavy paper sack. Stir with a stick. Pour the liquid ingredients on top of the dry ingredients. Gently stir the dough mixture until the dough rounds up into a ball. To cook, place a small ball of the dough mixture around a stick and cook over an open campfire. Let each camper cook his own.

Baking time varies. Cook until biscuit is browned on the outside and baked on the inside. This takes approximately five minutes, depending on the campfire size and the biscuit recipe used.

Take caution not to burn the biscuit. Remember a hot dog tastes fine when it is charcoaled on the outside, but a biscuit does not. Take special note these biscuits can be baked in an RV oven, if preferred. Simply follow our directions.

Directions For Rv Oven Biscuits:

Place dry ingredients in a mixing bowl. Stir and make a large hole in the dry ingredients. Pour liquid ingredients into the hole. Stir with fork until dough cleans the sides of the bowl and rounds up into a ball. Using one of the methods below, shape dough and place on a greased or nonstick cookie sheet.

Bake at 400 degrees F. in an RV oven for about 10 to 15 minutes or until biscuits are golden brown and done in center.

Shaping Methods For Rv Biscuits

Shaping dough is fun. If you want a super quick way to make the biscuits, use the Drop Biscuit method. Or want to get fancy? Shape the dough into Clover Leaf biscuits or Sailor's Knots. Or perhaps you have a special jam filling you want to bake into the biscuits. If that's the case, make Crescents.

Drop Biscuit Method: With a teaspoon, scoop a heaping portion of dough on the spoon and drop onto the greased or nonstick cookie sheet.

Clover Leaf Biscuits: Shape the dough into a roll about 9 inches long. To do this, roll dough as you would roll a stick or as you use a rolling pin with a back and forth motion. To keep the roll even, roll dough at center with both hands first and work your way to the ends. With a knife or scissors, cut the roll into 9 pieces. Next cut each piece into 3 smaller pieces. Take each of these small pieces and roll them into a little ball. After the 3 small pieces are rolled into little balls, place them by each other in a greased cup of a muffin pan.

Sailor's Knots Biscuits: Shape the dough into a roll about 9 inches long (refer to Clover Leaf Biscuits). With a knife or scissors, cut the roll into 9 pieces. Now roll each piece into the shape of a fat pencil about 6 inches long. Tie each piece into a loose knot; do not pull the knot hard or tight.

Crescents: Press the ball of dough into a flat shape. With a rolling pin, roll the dough into a circle about 1/2 inch thick. (For jam filling, spread it on the dough at this point.) With a knife, cut the circle dough like you would a pie into about 10 pieces. Roll each piece, starting at the wide end, around and around. Lightly pinch the end of the rolled dough together to keep it from unrolling.

Special note: Each following biscuit recipe makes about 10 to 12 biscuits.

BEST OLD - FASHIONED BUTTERMILK BISCUITS

2 cups white flour
2 teaspoons baking powder
1/4 teaspoon baking soda
1/3 cup vegetable oil
2/3 cup buttermilk

LUSCIOUS LEMON BISCUITS

1 cup soy flour
1 cup white flour
2½ teaspoons baking powder
1/2 teaspoon baking soda
1 tablespoon parsley flakes
1/3 cup vegetable oil
2/3 cup buttermilk
2 teaspoons lemon juice

TANGY ORANGE BISCUITS

1 cup white flour
1/2 cup soy flour
1/2 cup whole wheat flour
1 tablespoon baking powder
1 tablespoon grated orange rind
1 tablespoon sugar
1/4 cup vegetable oil
2/3 cup unsweetened orange juice

WHOLE WHEAT BISCUITS

3/4 cup whole wheat flour
1 cup white flour
1/4 cup wheat germ
3¼ teaspoons baking powder
1/3 cup vegetable oil
2/3 cup milk

SPECIAL SPICE BISCUITS

1/2 cup rye flour
1/2 cup whole wheat flour
1 cup white flour
1 teaspoon ginger
1 teaspoon cinnamon
1/4 teaspoon nutmeg
2½ teaspoons baking powder
1/2 teaspoon baking soda
2 tablespoons molasses
1/3 cup vegetable oil
2/3 cup buttermilk

APPETIZING APRICOT BISCUITS

1 cup white flour
1/2 cup soy flour
1/2 cup whole wheat flour
2 teaspoons baking powder
1/4 teaspoon baking soda
1/3 cup dried apricots, diced
1/3 cup vegetable oil
2/3 cup buttermilk

Chapter 20 **Try Muffins!**

Nothing draws campers to the camp table like the aroma of freshly baked muffins. And you will enjoy our tasty muffins that can be prepared in literally minutes. They can be baked in an RV or camp oven.

Like the biscuits, our muffin recipe directions are the same for each recipe. Only the ingredients vary. Simply follow our directions below.

Directions For Making Muffins:

Place dry ingredients in mixing bowl. Stir with a fork and make a hole in the dry ingredients. In another mixing bowl, stir liquid ingredients together. Pour liquid mixture into bowl of dry ingredients. Stir with fork just until ingredients are well mixed. Fill greased or nonstick muffin pans about two-thirds full. Bake in a 375 F. degree RV or camp oven for about 15 minutes or until muffins are browned and done in center. Each recipe makes about 10 muffins.

DELIGHTFUL BLUEBERRY MUFFINS

1½ cups white flour
1/2 cup soy flour
1 tablespoon baking powder
1 tablespoon sugar
1 egg, beaten
1 cup milk
1/2 cup fresh blueberries

BEST BRAN MUFFINS

2 cups white flour
1/2 cup bran cereal, crushed
2 teaspoons baking soda
1 teaspoon ginger
1/2 teaspoon cinnamon
1 egg, beaten
3 tablespoons molasses
1 cup sour milk
2 tablespoons vegetable oil

CLEVER CHERRY MUFFINS

2 cups white flour
1 tablespoon baking powder
1/2 cup instant cherry pie filling
1/2 cup milk
1 tablespoon honey

GREAT APPLE MUFFINS

1½ cups white flour
1/2 cup rye flour
1 tablespoon baking powder
1/4 teaspoon cloves
dash of nutmeg
1 tablespoon sugar
1/2 cup applesauce
1/2 cup milk
2 tablespoons vegetable oil

YUMMY CINNAMON MUFFINS

1½ cups white flour
1/2 cup whole wheat flour
1 tablespoon baking powder
1 tablespoon cinnamon
2 tablespoons sugar
1/2 cup walnuts
1 cup milk
1 tablespoon vegetable oil

Chapter 21   **Beer Breads? Baaaaatter Believe It!**

Sure, you love homemade bread but who wants to fuss all day at camp making bread? Wait a minute. Now you don't have to, not with our special super quick beer breads!

In minutes, these breads are ready for eating! There's no kneading, sifting or rising. Yet they taste delicious every time. All you need to do is stir the ingredients together and pour into a bread pan for baking. They couldn't be more simple to prepare. They're nutritious too. Sweetened with natural foods, they have no preservatives or additives.

For baking, an RV or camp oven is ideal. So is a Dutch oven set on hot coals. If you're using a Dutch over, make sure it is a 10 or 12 inch sized pan. That way the bread pan can set inside the Dutch oven pan with ample room around it for baking.

Set the bread pan on top of three or four hot coals, placed inside the Dutch over. Then cover the Dutch oven and set on top of a bed of hot coals. Also place some hot coals on top of the Dutch oven pan lid. To regulate the heat, use the coals on top of the Dutch oven. Simply add some coals for more heat or use less coals for a lower heat temperature.

Note: Like the biscuits and muffins, the preparation of these delicious beer breads is the same for all recipes. Only the ingredients vary. Simply follow the directions on the next page.

Directions For Beer Breads:

Place all the dry ingredients in a large mixing bowl. Pour in wet ingredients. Stir with a mixing spoon until ingredients are mixed. Pour bread batter in a regular-sized, greased or nonstick bread pan.

Bake in a 350 degree F. oven (RV oven, camp oven or Dutch oven) for approximately 45 minutes or until nicely browned and done in center. To test for doneness, tap center top of bread with finger. If bread sounds "hollow" it is baked throughout.

Want an extra quick bread? Make flat bread! To make flat bread, spread bread batter on a regular-sized greased or nonstick round pie plate; make batter about 1 inch in thickness. Bake in a 350 degree F. oven for about 20 minutes or until nicely browned and done in center.

If you're not familiar with beer breads, the texture of the baked breads is a lumpy top, not a smooth top like regular yeast breads.

BASIC BEER BREAD

3 cups self-rising flour
2 tablespoons sugar
1 12 ounce can beer

RYE BEER BREAD

2 cups self-rising flour
1 cup rye flour
1½ teaspoons baking powder
2 tablespoons molasses
1 12 ounce can beer

BEST EVER RAISIN BEER BREAD

2 cups self-rising flour
1/2 cup whole wheat flour
1/2 rye flour
1½ teaspoons baking powder
1 teaspoon cinnamon
1/2 teaspoon nutmeg
dash of cloves
3/4 cup raisins
1 tablespoon honey
1 12 ounce can beer

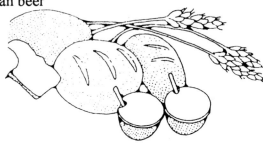

PARSLEY LEMON BEER BREAD

2 cups self-rising flour
1 cup soy flour
1½ teaspoons baking powder
2 tablespoons honey
1 tablespoon parsley flakes
1 tablespoon grated lemon rind
1 tablespoon lemon juice
1 12 ounce can beer

HEARTY DATE BEER BREAD

2 cups self-rising flour
1 cup whole wheat flour
1½ teaspoons baking powder
1 cup dates, chopped
1/4 cup prune juice
1 tablespoon honey
1 12 ounce can beer

APRICOT NUT BEER BREAD

2 cups self-rising flour
1 cup soy flour
1½ teaspoons baking powder
1/4 cup grape nut cereal
1 cup dried apricots, chopped
2 tablespoons honey
1 12 ounce can beer

Unit 8   Camping Projects

Chapter 22 Here's How To Clean Your Sleeping Bag!

How do you wash your sleeping bag? Do you throw it in your
washing machine? If you do, you probably hear the balance
buzzer ring every few minutes. Most home machines are not big
enough to handle a sleeping bag. Or, perhaps, you take your
bag to a Laundromat. This can be inconvenient, especially after
a camping trip. Or, maybe you send your bag to the cleaners.
That can be costly.

Have you ever thought of using your bathtub? No, I'm not
kidding. Take a look at your tub. It's the perfect place to wash
a sleeping bag. It's large, rectangular in shape and has a flat
surface. Even the largest, bulkiest sleeping bag will fit in it. A
tub is also convenient. The hot and cold water is at your
fingertips and, kneeling beside the tub, you have a nice working
level.

Using a bathtub gets the job done too. First, select the cleanser
you need, whether it be soap, detergent or shampoo.
To select a cleanser, read the label on your sleeping bag first to
see what fabric it contains. Then read the instructions on the
cleaner bottle. Are the two compatible? If the cleaner is not
suited for your sleeping bag, don't buy it. With all the
different cleaners on market, you will be able to find one suitable
for your sleeping bag. You can be sure of that. It's just a
matter of looking.

If your bag is filled with Dacron, use: a rug and upholstery
shampoo. The shampoo works well for washing sleeping bags.
This isn't as crazy as it sounds. Rug and upholstery shampoos

are designed for cleaning heavily soiled fabrics; sleeping bags, as all campers know, get heavily soiled.

Never use a detergent or shampoo on your bag if it's filled with down. Read the instructions on your bag to see what cleanser to use. As your instructions should tell you, detergent or shampoo will matte the down (form lumps) and will ruin the bag. After selecting the cleaner, place your sleeping bag in your bathtub and run about ten inches of lukewarm water in it. Pour as much cleaner in the water as the instructions specify.

Then use a drain plunger to clean your bag. I bought one to use just for cleaning sleeping bags. It was well worth the investment. It cost less than two dollars and, in one washing, paid for itself. A plunger gives your bag gentle, thorough cleaning and doesn't cause the sleeping bag fibers to matte. It's easy to use but don't pound it. This is unnecessary. Use a slow, steady motion to force the water and soap through the sleeping bag gently. You should see your water getting dirty when you do this.

After cleaning your bag with the plunger, drain the water and rinse. When rinsing, it's important to get all the soap out. Residue soap left on the bag will draw moisture, accumulate dirt and can irritate the skin. It's not hard to get the soap out. Simply pull the plug and let as much water drain as possible. Then roll the bag in a corner of the tub. Don't attempt to lift the bag. A wet sleeping bag may weigh up to sixty pounds. That means, if it was picked up at this weight, seams could rip and fabric could tear from the pressure. Let the bag drain in this rolled position for five or ten minutes. After the water is fairly well drained from the bag, it's ready for the first rinse.

Fill the tub with cold water. Cold water gets soap out of the fibers more quickly and thoroughly than warm water. You used a plunger to get the soap in the bag to clean it. Don't stop now.

Use the plunger to get the soap out of the bag to rinse it. Use the same slow motion. Rinse the bag one or two times by this procedure. When you can't see any soap suds come out of the sleeping bag when you use the plunger, the bag is well rinsed.

How do you hang a sixty-pound wet sleeping bag? You don't.

Remember you shouldn't lift it at this weight. So, you put your sleeping bag on a crash diet. To do this, drain it once more in the rolled position at the high end of the tub. Then partially lift the bag by one corner and hold for two or three minutes. To continue drainage, grip the bag on opposite sides and slowly raise full length. It may be necessary to drape the bag over your arm and support the weight of the bag by gripping a towel rack with one hand. In a few seconds, you'll see your bag loose 30 or 40 pounds. This diet is quick, effective and safe for sleeping bags.

Your bag should now weigh between 14 and 20 pounds. Put it in a laundry basket and carry to the clothes line. Space clothes pins about eight inches apart and let the bag dry. This won't take as long as you may think. My sleeping bags dry in one day, if the sun is out. If the weather is overcast, it takes two or three days.

When you bring your bag in from the line, don't roll it up as you would for a camping trip. Fold it. It stores much better this way because the fibers are not rolled tightly together which means less wear and tear on your bag.

That's it. Your bag is now in your closet, smelling fresh and clean--ready for winter storage or your next camping trip.

Chapter 23   How To Make An Inexpensive Child's Backpack

Tired of carrying your child's backpacking supplies on those camping trips? Good news! With a towel and a couple of washcloths you can make your child a sturdy backpack. No joke.

With these inexpensive materials, you can make your child a backpack so both you and your child can hike with ease. No longer will you need to overload your backpack with extra beach towels, small swimming suits, shoes and socks, dead bugs and rock and flower collections. Our child's backpack has ample room for even the most active camping child.

Besides providing plenty of space, this backpack is comfortable for children. The straps are altered for individual children's sizes. The main backpack itself is measured, cut and tailored especially for a child's body.

And don't let the tailoring scare you. Even a beginner seamstress can make this child's backpack easily. The following instructions are simple and thorough.

Materials:
To begin the backpack, get a terry cloth towel that measures 20½ inches by 36 inches in size. All the backpack pieces, except the pocket and pocket flap, are cut from the towel.

For the pocket and pocket flap, use two regular-sized wash cloths or two potholders. Personally, I like to use potholders. The thick potholder fabric gives extra insulation, making the backpack pocket great for carrying a child's thermos jug. Select a cotton-covered polyester thread for sewing. It's extra durable.

Cutting directions:

Starting from either long side of the towel, measure and cut two long strips. Make each of them 4½ inches wide and the length of the towel.

Cut the two strips again, making the inserts and straps. Simply cut 13 inches off each strip. The two 13 inch strips are the inserts. The remaining two strips, measuring 4¼ inches by 23 inches are the straps.

The last piece of the towel measures 12 inches by 36 inches and is the main backpack. This piece is folded to make the back, front, bottom and top flap of the backpack.

Making the folds:

To make the appropriate folds in the backpack piece when sewing, mark them first. Start by measuring 13 inches down from either of the short 12-inch hemmed towel edges and draw a chalk line across. Don't cut this. This fold makes the front of the backpack.

Next, measure 4 inches farther down from the chalk line and draw another chalk line across this backpack piece. Don't cut here either. This fold shapes the bottom of the backpack.

Make a third chalk line, measuring 13 inches from the second chalk line. Don't cut this line either. This folds to make the back of the backpack (where the straps will be attached). The remaining 6 inches of the towel backpack piece is the top flap of the backpack.

Sewing directions:

Sew the pocket to the backpack front. The backpack front, remember, is the 13-inch measured space from the top end of the main backpack piece.

To begin the pocket, pin one of the washcloths 5 inches from the top hemmed towel edge of the front of the backpack. Center this washcloth horizontally, so there's the same amount of towel on each of the washcloth sides.

Notice the washcloth has finished edges, so overcasting raw edges isn't necessary. Simply top stitch the washcloth to the front of the backpack on your sewing machine, using a regular machine straight stitch. This is about 10 to 12 stitches per inch.

Sew near just the three outer washcloth edges, the sides and the bottom, leaving the top edge open. The open top of the washcloth edge makes the pocket opening.

With the other washcloth, make a flap for the already sewn washcloth pocket. To do this, lay the bottom edge of the unsewn washcloth right beside the top open edge of the sewn washcloth pocket. Machine top stitch only the edge near the top of the pocket. The other three sides are left to flap over the sewn pocket as needed.

If desired, use a zigzag machine stitch to sew this edge. A zigzag here gives maximum strength and durability for turning the flap over the pocket.

Use one of the several methods for holding the pocket and flap together. A large button and buttonhole work well. Large snaps may be used. Strips of a touch fastener material, such as Velcro © can be sewn to attach the flap to the pocket. These fastener materials are available in most fabric and department stores.

After completing the pocket and pocket flap, sew the straps. Fold each of the two cut strap pieces in half lengthwise. Pin the raw edges together on both strap pieces. Machine straight stitch these edges, leaving both the top and bottom short strap ends open. Use a ¼ inch seam.

After sewing this seam on each strap, turn both straps inside out so the raw seam edges turn to the inside and don't show. This prevents raw fiber edges from raveling and ripping the long sewn seam apart. Press both straps flat with a warm iron.

Next, overcast the raw edges of each of the bottom strap ends. The top ends of the strap don't need overcasting because the original hemmed towel edges are on these ends. Sew the overcasted bottom ends of the strap to the back of the backpack. Remember, the back of the backpack is the measured 13 inch space between the backpack bottom fold line and the backpack top flap fold line.

To attach the bottoms of the strap ends to the backpack, first place the straps on the right side of the backpack piece. The right side is the same side of the towel on which the pocket and flap are sewn at the other end of the backpack front.

Pin each strap about two inches above the bottom of the backpack fold line and an inch or two from each of the backpack side edges. Using a straight machine stitch, sew a 1½ inch square near each bottom strap end.

Sew through all three fabric layers, two strap layers, and one backpack layer. Then sew an X in the middle of each square, again stitching through the three fabric layers. This stitched square makes the straps extra durable--as they need to be for supporting a loaded backpack properly.

Don't sew the top strap ends to the backpack yet. Instead, make the side inserts. Then the backpack can be tried on a child for size and the straps sewn accordingly.

To sew the inserts, work with one side at a time. First pin one of the insert cut pieces to one of the long sides of the front of the backpack, starting at the top. Match the hemmed towel edges of the front of the backpack with the hemmed towel edges of the insert and pin right sides together.

Notice the insert piece is much shorter in length than the front of the backpack. This is because the entire main backpack piece (front, back and bottom) is folded, pinned, and sewed to three sides of the insert.

Machine stitch the first insert seam from the matched and pinned hemmed towel edges at the top to 5/8 inch from the insert bottom edge. With a scissors, clip through both the backpack and insert pieces diagonally, pointing to the bottom of the seam. Make the clip about ½ inch long.

Next, measure 4 inches farther down from the clip on the backpack side edge and make another diagonal clip in the backpack. Then clip the insert diagonally again, parallel to the clip already made to the insert.

These clips allow the main backpack and side inserts to stretch and turn. Turning the insert as needed, pin the bottom to the measured off 4 inches on the backpack. Machine stitch this seam, making the bottom of the backpack. Again stop 5/8 inch from the insert edge.

Next, turn the insert piece and pin the remaining long edge of the insert to the remaining raw edge of the backpack piece, leaving the towel edge overhang for the flap of the backpack. There will be approximately six inches of overhang.

Sew this last side insert seam, having the hemmed towel edges match again with the side inserts hemmed towel edge. This seam is parallel to the first sewn insert seam.

Notice how the sewn insert makes the backpack side. Sew the other cut insert piece, exactly the same way, to make the other side of the backpack.

Next, finish the backpack flap.

To do this, hem the two long edges of the measured flap piece. Either double turn these edges and sew a straight machine stitch, or single turn and sew a zigzag stitch or, if you have a serger, simply serge the ends. Any of the methods will enclose the edges nicely and gives a professional appearance.

After hemming the backpack flap edges, sew two long strips of touch fastener material to fasten the flap of the backpack to the backpack itself.

This is done by simply sewing one touch fastener strip near the bottom edge of the backpack flap on the wrong side, which lays against the backpack. Sew the other touch fastener strip near the top edges of the front of the backpack.

To complete the backpack, adjust the straps to fit the child. A child's backpack straps should be loose for comfort but snug enough not to fall off the shoulders. After adjusting the straps, attach the top strap ends to the backpack.

Pin the strap tops at an angle by placing them several inches from the backpack measured fold line and several inches from the backpack sides. The angle makes the straps easy for children to wear and manage. The backpack will not slip off the child's back and will be more comfortable than if the straps were sewn straight. Sew the strap tops to the backpack, using the same stitched square used on the bottom strap ends.

Laundry directions:

To wash the backpack, simply toss in warm or even hot sudsy water in a washing machine. Any laundry detergent works well. Wash on a normal wash and rinse cycle. Dry in an automatic dryer on a warm setting or hang on a clothes line.

Chapter 24   Tips To Keep Camp Kids Happy

"I'm bored!"

Sound familiar? It's not uncommon for children to get bored at times when they're camping. But now they don't have to be! Take a look at our tips which include activities to involve children in the camping experience.

*Make a bug cage. Make a bug cage with an empty milk carton or iced tea mix can and an old nylon stocking. Simply cut a couple large holes on the side of the milk carton or iced tea mix can with a scissors. Then cut off one leg of an old pair of pantyhose. Next slip the stocking over the milk carton and presto! you've got a bug cage. Kids can capture insects at camp by tossing them in the completed bug cage and then tying a knot at the opened end of the cut stocking. That way youngsters can view and study the insects by looking through the nylon-covered windows.

*Collect rocks. Children love to put different-sized rocks in a box and play with them or polish them for display somewhere-- perhaps a science fair project or a scouting experience.

*Take nature hikes. Take your children on a hike to enjoy the scenery. Point out interesting things to them and let them point out interesting things to you. It's fun to take a hike and observe things from a child's point of view.

*Build a sand or mud castle. Any campsite is good for building castles. There's always sand or dirt available and this can capture a child's interest for a long time.

*Read books. Wait a minute, you may be saying, read a book outdoors? Why not? Children enjoy books outdoors under a shady tree or while sunning themselves. For your next trip with kids, take several of the youngster's favorite books and perhaps a new one for them to enjoy outside.

*Make snacks. Camp kids get hungry, hungry, hungry. Let them make their own snacks. Have cereals, nuts and dried fruits on hand for mixing and placing in small plastic bags. For a special treat, kids can poke some banana and apple slices on toothpicks for mini-kebabs. Keep a loaf of bread and a jar of peanut butter handy for kids to make between meal sandwiches.

*Pick wild flowers. Children appreciate nature when they can pick a handful of wild flowers and put them in a vase. Don't have a vase at the campsite? Make one by cleaning a paper milk carton and cover with a pretty stick-on paper that can be purchased in most grocery and department stores. Or, if desired, the flowers can be dried--also another good scouting or science fair project.

*Make arrangements to attend a ranger program, if possible, when camping. Introduce your youngsters to the forest rangers that are available. Rangers enjoy pointing out safety tips to kids and telling them about the fun spots at their particular camp.

*Make a list of the different kinds of birds at camp. Children are eager to learn about nature. Supply your kids with paper and pencil and recommend they note the different birds they see while camping. Have them jot down the color, size and special characteristics of the birds.

*Gather sticks for cooking. Kids often want to cook hot dogs or marshmallows over an open campfire but often don't have the sticks available. Have them collect sticks ahead of time at camp. With a grown-ups help, they can sharpen the sticks one end with a jack knife.

*Make a batch of play dough. Play dough is fun for youngsters but it can be messy indoors. So let your kids make a batch of play dough outdoors and enjoy! Here's how: Mix 1½ cups flour, 2/3 cup salt and 1 tablespoon cream of tartar in a large mixing bowl. Add 2/3 cup water and 3 tablespoons vegetable oil. Stir until ingredients are well mixed. Divide mixture and color with food coloring, as desired, by squirting some drops of a food color--blue, yellow, red or green--into the dough and mix thoroughly with hands. If you want to get some other colors, do so accordingly:

For orange: squirt 2 drops of red and 3 drops of yellow into mixture and mix with hands. For turquoise: squirt 1 drop of green with 4 drops of blue into dough mixture and mix with hands. For red salmon: squirt 3 drops of red and 2 drops of yellow into dough mixture and mix with hands. For mint green: squirt 1 drop of yellow and 4 drops of green into dough mixture and mix with hands. For purple: squirt 2 drops of red and 2 drops of blue into dough mixture and mix with hands. If you want darker colors, simply double the squirts accordingly. For lighter colors, decrease the squirts accordingly.

*Make a bird feeder. Have your children cut the bottom from an old cardboard box, leaving one or two inch height sides. Tear a couple bread slices into tiny pieces. Spread bread pieces in cardboard box feeder. Set somewhere on the campsite and see how your feeder and food attract different birds.

*Make finger paints. Finger paints are lots of fun for kids-- especially camp kids. Help them make some. Here's how. Place 1/3 cup cornstarch in a medium-sized saucepan. Add 1½ cups water, a little at a time, to the cornstarch while stirring with a mixing spoon; stir well until water and cornstarch are mixed. Then cook the mixture over a low to medium camp fire or RV range until the mixture comes to a boil. Stir the mixture continuously until it thickens. Generally, this takes about 6 to 8 minutes. Next remove from heat. Add 3 tablespoons talcum powder and 3 tablespoons of a mild liquid dish washing soap. Stir until mixed. Next pour and divide the mixture into several or more paper cups. To color, see above directions in play dough recipe.

There. These ideas will keep camp kids entertained and insure that they have an enjoyable experience. With our tips, bet your kids no longer will say, "I'm bored!"

About the author

Experimental cookery was Mary Ann Heimbuch's favorite course in college. She decided then to write food articles and cookbooks some day.

A South Dakota native, Mary Ann graduated from South Dakota State University with B.S. degrees in Home Economics and Journalism with a Natural Science minor. Three days after graduating, she married Bob Kerl, also an SDSU alumni, and began writing and selling food articles to *Family Circle, Lady's Circle, Women's Comfort, Women's Household, Virtue* and other national publications.

She enjoys experimenting with recipes in her McAlester, Oklahoma home where she has resided with her husband since the late 1970's.

Presently Mary Ann is a correspondent for The Daily Oklahoman newspaper in Oklahoma City and served the same position previously with Tulsa World for thirteen years. She has received over 40 national writing awards and has published over 1,500 articles and stories.

Other published royalty books include *Breads, Breads, Breads!* that features heart-smart breads, also published by Quioxte Press. Two books by LangMarc Publishing are titled *Are You Listening, Lord?*, for teen girls, and *Angel On Trial*, a humorous fantasy for adults. *Where Are You, Lord?*, for young girls, was in Augsburg Fortress' best-selling series—Books for Young Readers.

Need A Gift?

For

• Shower • Birthday • Mother's Day •
• Anniversary • Christmas •

Turn Page for Order Form

<u>TO ORDER COPIES OF:</u>

Camp Cookin'

Please send me _____copies at $9.95 each plus $3.50 S/H each. (Make checks payable to **HEARTS N' TUMMIES COOKBOOK CO.**)

Name _____

Street _____

City _____ State _____ Zip _____

SEND ORDERS TO:
HEARTS 'N TUMMIES
3544 Blakslee Street
Wever, IA 52658
800-571-2665

-- -- -- -- -- -- -- -- -- -- -- -- -- -- --

<u>TO ORDER COPIES OF:</u>

Camp Cookin'

Please send me _____copies at $9.95 each plus $3.50 S/H each. (Make checks payable to **HEARTS N' TUMMIES COOKBOOK CO.**)

Name _____

Street _____

City _____ State _____ Zip _____

SEND ORDERS TO:
HEARTS 'N TUMMIES
3544 Blakslee Street
Wever, IA 52658
800-571-2665

1

2

See p. 17

3

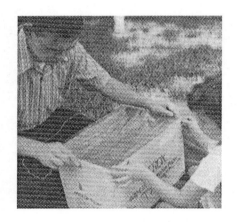

4

5

See p. 21

See p. 22

149

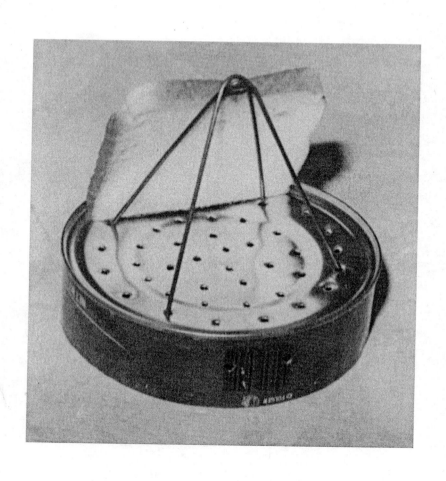

See p. 23